TRADITIONAL NEEDLE ARTS

RIBBONCRAFT

TRADITIONAL NEEDLE ARTS

RIBBONCRAFT

More than 20 classic projects

DEENA BEVERLEY

PHOTOGRAPHY BY TIM IMRIE

MITCHELL BEAZLEY

For Carole

First published in Great Britain in 1997
by Mitchell Beazley,
an imprint of Reed Consumer Books Limited
Michelin House, 81 Fulham Road,
London SW3 6RB
and Auckland, Melbourne, Singapore and Toronto

Editor	**JULIA NORTH**
Senior Art Editor	**SUSAN DOWNING**
Photographic Art Director/	
Stylist	**DEENA BEVERLEY**
Designer	**MERYL JAMES**
Production	**JULIETTE BUTLER**
Illustrations	**KEVIN HART**
Templates	**KUO KANG CHEN**
Executive Editor	**JUDITH MORE**
Executive Art Editor	**JANIS UTTON**
Art Director	**GAYE ALLEN**

A CIP record for this book is available from the
British Library

ISBN 1 85732 789 6

The publishers have made every effort to ensure that
all instructions given in this book are accurate and safe
but they cannot accept liability for any resulting injury,
damage or loss to either person or property, whether
direct or consequential and howsoever arising.

The author and publishers will be grateful for any
information which will assist them in keeping future
editions up to date.

Typeset in Perpetua 12/16 and 10/12pt
Index compiled by Hilary Bird
Produced by Mandarin Offset

Printed and bound in Hong Kong

Contents

Introduction

Ribbons have been used since the Middle Ages to embellish both clothing and soft furnishings. The word ribbon simply means "a narrow strip of cloth".

Being so closely allied to garment design, ribbon manufacture has always been a fickle and unstable trade – enslaved to the winds of fashion, and blighted at various times throughout its history by social and economic changes, as well as the idiosyncrasies of changing tastes. Failure of silkworm crops, wars and trade embargoes have all at various times taken their toll.

In the late 17th century, however, demand for ribbons was intense, filtering through fashionable society from the elaborate ribbon rosettes, ruched edgings and lavish bows worn in the French court. The ribbon industry centred upon France, particularly around Lyons, Paris and Saint Etienne, but production also developed in other cities including Basle in Switzerland, Vienna in Austria, Krefeld in Germany, and Coventry in England.

Each area had its own speciality, although inevitably there was a gradual cross-pollination of ideas and techniques. Saint Etienne produced brilliantly detailed woven jacquard designs incorporating silver and gold lamé in the threads. The looms on which such ribbons were produced took weeks to set up, making the end product extremely expensive. Nonetheless, demand was great, and Saint Etienne exported worldwide. Conversely, plain ribbons were the speciality of Basle, and were imported to Saint Etienne.

In England, silk ribbon production began in the 17th century, as the Huguenot weavers fled from France. Coventry became the

RIGHT The chrysanthemums worked in ombré silk ribbon on this early religious piece show very clearly how realistic sculptural ribbon embroidery can be.

centre of the British ribbon industry and at one time a quarter of all its inhabitants were employed solely in ribbon manufacture. Initially, these ribbons were produced chiefly by outworkers, but with the advent of steam, factory production slowly took over.

The Jacquard loom, in use in France since 1801, revolutionized ribbon weaving. Capable of producing incredibly detailed designs, use of this loom slowly spread to other countries, and new uses for Jacquard ribbons were developed. Black and white drawings translated well into woven silk, and many souvenir pictures were made and sold at exhibitions and important events.

ABOVE Early 19th-century ribbon embroidery was largely confined to domestic items such as needlecases.

However, ribbons were still used predominantly to trim the clothes of both men and women, rather than featuring in interior decoration. This was not a uniquely European fashion. In North America, needles, scissors and thread were already being widely used as trade items with the Native Americans Indians when silk ribbon arrived from Europe around 1800.

The Native Americans of the woodlands and the Eastern plains used these ribbons in a very different way to the flamboyant gathers and frills popular elsewhere. Clear, bright primary colours were favoured, as opposed to the delicate watercolour palette of European taste. They cut geometric patterns into one ribbon, then appliquéd this to a ribbon in a contrasting colour. Several strips were worked in this way, then joined to make decorative panels which were appliquéd to skirts, robes, leggings and moccasins.

Ribbon embroidery at this time was generally confined to small domestic items such as pincushions and needlecases, and was known as China ribbon embroidery. Stitches were worked using narrow China ribbons, no wider than 1.5mm ($^{1}/_{16}$in), in place of thread. The ribbons – some plain, some shaded – were combined with stitches in chenille and embroidery silks to produce brightly coloured and beautifully textural designs. The same ribbons were also threaded through underwear, used to decorate childrens' dresses, and employed as bookmarks. In the late 1880s, China ribbon embroidery, having suffered a temporary decline in interest, enjoyed a revival, and subsequently became known as Rococo work. French-influenced designs were numerous, especially those featuring a simple posy of flowers, depicted either in a basket or tied with a ribbon bow.

Increasingly, Rococo work became popular as a way of enlivening all manner of domestic furnishings, such as mats, picture frames, sachets, runners and firescreens. The craft was popular worldwide, and then, as now, specialist mail order companies developed to cater for the passion. Special ribbons were developed, such as picotee, literally meaning "pinked". This ribbon was 15mm ($^{5}/_{8}$in) wide and serrated along one edge. When gathered along the remaining edge, it was perfect for recreating realistic carnations, or pinks, which were then attached to the ground fabric with tiny thread stitches. Another popular ribbon was giant crepe, which had a delicately crinkled surface ideal for making poppies. Ribbon flowers were sometimes constructed individually in this way, and sometimes embroidered directly through the cloth,

ABOVE This glorious pelmet, with its rich gold bullion trim, is a wonderful example of Rococo work.

composed from individual stitches of ribbon. Both types of work were often employed within a single piece, and combining the two techniques is a practise that continues in contemporary ribbon embroidery.

The diversity and subtlety of Rococo work is quite astonishing. My only difficulty in producing this book was in deciding which pieces of ribbon embroidery were to be omitted. I found examples at all skill levels absolutely irresistible; from quite clumsily wrought student pieces to the amazingly complex detail on the religious examples. The chrysanthemum motif on the chair back on page 78 is a wonderful example of the effects that can be achieved by a combination of using shaded ribbons and careful manipulation of the ribbon on the surface of the fabric into realistic petal shapes. The expense and luxury of silk ribbons, often combined with pure gold and silver threads, has long rendered them appropriate for use in items of royal or religious significance. The quality of stitching on these ecclesiastical pieces is simply faultless; recalling the Shaker maxim of "hands to work, hearts to God".

There is a sharp division between this sort of intricate work, which features very narrow ribbons, extremely finely wrought, and the pieces worked in wider ribbons, often using simple, straight stitches to produce effective designs much more quickly. Both are quite charming in different ways, and I found the naïveté of some of the designs tremendously encouraging in my first hesitant forays into Rococo work. Even an inexperienced embroiderer can produce deceptively complex results almost instantaneously.

Many of the examples in this book date from the Victorian era, since ribbons were used in all kinds of ingenious ways at this time to make useful and beautiful soft furnishings. In England, patchwork quilts were made from scraps of ribbon collected from weavers' ends. English quilts were also made in the traditionally American design of log cabin patchwork, using wide silk millinery ribbons. Victorian ladies extended their astonishing range of creative pastimes into painting on ribbons. Ribbons were first embroidered in place, then delicately coloured using watercolours or oil paints to create shaded effects.

ABOVE The gold threads and silk ribbons on this chair back, originally part of a religious garment, combine in another faultlessly executed piece of Rococo work.

Silk ribbons have been used throughout history to add sumptuous detail to items intended for everyday use, as well as pieces designed for special occasions. Today, affordable synthetic alternatives are more widely available than silks, though silk types can be bought from specialist suppliers (see page 128). Modern innovative designs can be used to create wonderfully dramatic results. Wire-edged ribbons can be sculpted into amazing bows and garlands that will hold their shape indefinitely. Even the simplest bow tied in wide, wire-edged ribbon and tweaked into shape gives a professional-looking finish to a bouquet or dried flower arrangement. Just a short length of wire-edged ribbon twined around a plain wreath of holly or ivy and finished in a bow gives a glamourous flourish to a front door at Christmas time.

Ribbons are a wonderful way of enlivening all areas of the home, with minimal expenditure of time and effort. This is particularly useful nowadays, when the demands of our busy modern lifestyle often threaten to engulf the simpler pleasures in life. The marketplace has been quick to exploit this renewed interest in ribbon embroidery. New stitches, techniques and materials are constantly being introduced – and spread through specialist shops, books, mail order companies and classes. Most general needlework suppliers stock a good range of narrow ribbons.

During the course of producing this book, I have been fortunate enough to have handled and examined some marvellous examples of ribboncraft. My imagination has been fired by all sorts of new applications for these delightful "narrow strips of cloth". I hope that some of this enthusiasm for ribboncraft, inspired by generations of needle workers, will be transferred into your own repertoire of needle arts skills.

ABOVE Whether filmy organza or glossy and resilient satin, ribbon roses hold their shape beautifully and have been used for centuries to decorate everything from hats to tie-backs.

Before you begin

The projects included in this book are all derived from traditional pieces of ribboncraft of various disciplines. There are projects suitable for all ability levels, using a variety of techniques, from ribbon embroidery to ribbon patchwork. All the projects have been carefully researched for both historical accuracy and translation into contemporary materials and methods where appropriate.

It is well worth reading this section carefully, particularly if you are new to ribboncraft. A thorough understanding of the basic techniques at the outset will ensure consistently satisfying results.

Within this section, you will find descriptions and illustrations of all the stitches and techniques required to complete every project in this book.

BASIC REQUIREMENTS

All the projects in this book require the usual range of needlework tools and materials.

Appropriate choices of the items marked with an asterisk* are critical to the success of the finished work.

Requirements include
- Ribbon*
- Fabric*
- Thread*
- Needles*
- Embroidery hoop or frame (optional)*
- Dressmaker's marking pencils or pens
- Embroidery scissors
- Good light source (daylight or daylight bulb)
- Clean, dry hands
- Cards and tubes on which to store ribbon**
- Dressmaker's transfer paper
- Tracing paper

** Store narrow silk ribbons on small rolled cards such as business cards. Fix the cards with adhesive tape and cut a slot in each end to prevent the ribbon unravelling. Do not wind ribbons around flat cards. Silk ribbons in particular will develop creases if stored wound flat.

Ribbons
You can purchase ribbons in a staggering array of textures, widths, colours and patterns. They divide broadly into two categories: woven-edge and craft. Woven-edge ribbons are lengths of fabric that have been especially woven to specific widths. These are generally suitable for applications that require laundering, though you should always check the reel on which the ribbon is sold for full care instructions.

Craft ribbons are simply strips of fabric that have been cut from a wider piece, and treated with a special finish to prevent fraying. This finish would be removed by washing. For most stitched applications, as in this book, craft ribbons are not suitable, so check carefully that your ribbon has two woven selvedges before purchasing.

13

Wire-edged ribbons are also now widely available, and are perfect for constructing elaborate bows for display purposes only, since most are not washable. It is possible to remove the wire from the edges of some ribbons, as on the shopping basket (page 99) to achieve a softer, less theatrical look.

Needles

Accurate choice of the right needle is essential to the success of ribbon embroidery. For ribbon embroidery the needle must make a hole of sufficient size in the fabric for the ribbon to pass through easily, so that it can spread out on the surface of the fabric. When first using the correct size of needle, you will probably be alarmed at the size of the hole punctured in the fabric, but the ribbon will spread comfortably as it passes through the hole, and will cover it completely. If the ribbon does not spread out easily on the surface, try using a larger needle.

Crewel embroidery needles are suited to most fabrics when using 4mm/⅛in width silk ribbon. A mixed pack including sizes 1-5 should be adequate for most applications. The eye of the needle must also be sufficiently large to allow the ribbon to lie perfectly flat when threaded. A mixed pack of chenille needles, sizes 18-24, will be suitable for 7mm/¼in width ribbons. For threading ribbon through eyelets, or wrapping ribbon around base stitches, use a blunt-ended tapestry needle. For general needlework and making-up, a pack of medium-sized "Sharp" needles will be useful.

Threads

There are many types of thread that are used in ribboncraft – including silks, synthetics, and cottons. For most embroidery projects in this book, silk thread has been specified, as this was the thread used on the antique pieces before the advent of synthetics. As a rule, choose a thread that is suited to the most important part of your work so that it will stand the test of time. The thread needs to be fine and strong enough to be secure, yet not so strong that it will cut through delicate fibres such as silk ribbons in years to come, after repeated use and laundering.

Fine cotton thread is an affordable alternative, and synthetic threads may be used with synthetic ribbons. Synthetic threads may also be used with silk ribbons, but since these are a relatively new innovation, it is not certain how they will perform in the long term. Stranded cotton, metallic threads, coton perlé (pearl cotton) and other embroidery threads are also specified throughout the book to give results as close as possible to the original pieces.

Embroidery frames

Most people find it easier to work evenly when the base fabric is held securely in place. This is important where it is essential to the design that the ribbon spreads on the surface of the fabric. Take care that the hoop does not mark the fabric, especially when using velvet. A small (8 or 9cm/3 or 3½in diameter) plastic frame is ideal for most projects. If using a wooden hoop, wrap it in strips of fabric so that it does not snag the work.

FABRICS FOR RIBBONCRAFT

Almost any material can be used as a base for ribboncrafts, but all the items in this book were made from different natural fabrics such as calico, silk, cotton or linen. Many of the pieces featured date from the mid-19th century, when silk was widely used in ribboncrafts. For silk ribbon embroidery, choose a background fabric relevant to the end use of the project. For example, the ribbon-embroidered tablecloth has been worked on linen, which will withstand frequent laundering; but the delicate embroidery on the shoe trees has been stitched onto a precious scrap of Georgian silk, since regular cleaning will not be needed.

Remember that the materials selected will dictate the wash temperature of the finished piece, which need to be washed according to the most delicate fibre; for example, silk ribbons would not be suitable for embroidery on a towel, as the towel would require much higher temperatures and stronger detergents than the silk ribbons could tolerate.

Ribbon embroidery is most successful when worked on an evenly woven fabric that has neither a very loose nor very tight weave. Most dress fabrics are suitable, including synthetics, velvet, voile and most natural fabrics. When working on stretch fabrics, back the material with a firm fabric such as organza and mount the work in a hoop so that the ribbons sit evenly.

Some people like to back fabrics for ribbon embroidery with fine, iron-on interfacing. This has several advantages. The surface fabric remains smooth and easy to mount or make up into a finished article; ribbon ends on the back of the work are not visible on the front (particularly important when using a fine surface fabric such as *voile*), and marks left by an embroidery hoop are minimized. If you are embroidering with velvet ribbon, and are pulling it through the fabric, choose a slightly looser woven fabric than usual; for example linen, cotton, or wool. If these fabrics are unsuitable, use the velvet ribbon on the surface of the fabric only, secured in place with tiny stitches.

RIBBON TEXTURES

An astonishing range of fibres is used to create a multitude of ribbon textures, from filmy organdies to sumptuous velvets.

Satin ribbon is available either single-face (shiny on one side only) or double-face (shiny on both sides). Its deep sheen adds irresistible glamour, even when used simply and in small quantities.

Grosgrains, traditionally used in millinery, are very resilient with a dense, ribbed weave. Tough and hard-wearing, they have been used to wrap the handle of the ribbon rose-trimmed basket (see page 94), as they will withstand years of handling. Their distinctive appearance is a sophisticated foil for the more feminine textures of silk and lace.

Velvet ribbons are usually textured on one side only, but occasionally may be found double-faced. Treated to prevent fraying, their rich pile makes realistic flowers, as on the pansy nightdress case (see page 58).

Organdies, traditionally made from silk, are now mostly synthetic in origin. Sheer and fine, they are widely used in flower-making, and applications where a delicate, romantic effect is required, as in the ribbon roses on the silk and lace basket (on page 94).

Jacquard ribbons owe their name to Monsieur Joseph Marie Jacquard,

inventor of the Jacquard loom that revolutionized the ribbon industry in the late 18th century. The loom produces complex woven designs, such as the madder-coloured ribbon used to edge one of the traditional blankets.

Silk ribbons are incomparable for use in ribbon embroidery, particularly if you wish to achieve an authentic appearance consistent with the antique examples in this book. Ombré ribbons (shaded across the width from light to dark) are worth seeking out, as they give a marvellous quality to the finished embroidery. If you cannot find narrow silk ombré ribbons, experiment with the dyeing and painting instructions in this section to achieve satisfying results. Although synthetic alternatives are now available, they are too springy to fold and drape convincingly into the naturalistic flower shapes that are so typical of 19th-century ribbon embroidery. However, sometimes this ebullient nature is very useful, as in the ribbons that are woven through the white companion cushion (on page 65).

Simple cotton tapes are also used to great effect when pleated or gathered into decorative edgings and floral motifs, as in the tape lace curtains and tie-backs (on page 22).

Military wool tapes are hard-wearing and have a comforting, substantial feel. They are a cosy way of adding visual interest and practical reinforcement to utilitarian designs.

Technological advances mean that new textures and fibres of ribbon are constantly being introduced. By substituting these exciting variants, you can change the look of the projects in this book entirely. Pleated velvets, luminous taffetas,

picot-edged jacquards, are just a few of the temptations in store.

SEWING WITH RIBBON

Pay particular attention to selecting the right size and type of needle for your work. If you use too small a needle, the ribbon may fray as it is forced through an inadequately sized hole in the fabric, as well as making mean and thin stitches. Read the paragraph on needle selection for further details.

Starting and finishing

Threading: Use only short lengths of ribbon (30cm/12in) when embroidering. Longer pieces of silk ribbon will deteriorate through being overworked, and are difficult to manipulate easily. Thread the ribbon through the eye of the needle, then, using the needle tip, pierce the centre of the ribbon 6mm/¼in from the end which you have just threaded. Pull the long end of the ribbon tightly to lock it securely onto the needle (see illustration on page 17).

To begin a stitch: Fold the end of the ribbon over onto itself and pierce the fold with the needle tip. Pull the remaining ribbon through to leave a loop at the end. This produces a soft knot that remains on the back of the work.

To finish: With the ribbon on the underside of the fabric, lay the ribbon across an adjacent stitch and stitch twice through both ribbons. Snip the ribbon close to this double knot. If you are hesitant about producing a knot on the reverse of your work, or you are working with synthetic ribbons that may not be held securely by this method, leave a tail 1.5cm/½in long on the back of the work, and hold down with tiny back stitches in thread. Alternatively, weave the end of the ribbon through adjacent stitches on the back of the work. If you need to press the finished embroidery, do so very lightly on the reverse, working on a well-padded surface; for example a few layers of white cotton fabric wrapped around a folded towel.

GETTING THE TENSION RIGHT

To prevent the ribbon twisting as you stitch, hold the flat ribbon under your left thumb as you pull the needle through to the reverse of the work. Any twists should now pass through the fabric before you remove your thumb, leaving a flat, smooth loop to form a stitch. When pulling the ribbon through the fabric, handle it very gently and let it find its own place. The ribbon must be allowed to spread comfortably to its full width on the surface of the fabric for a satisfactory result.

SIZEING AND DYING

Since Victorian times, ribbons have been dyed and painted at home to produce natural-looking shades similar to those of real flowers.

Some ribbons have actually been chemically treated during manufacture in such a way that prevents home dyes adhering smoothly. Even natural oils in the cleanest finger tips can jeopardize the result, so before starting colouring, use a permeation solution. Mix two cups of lukewarm water with two drops of washing-up liquid in a small bowl. Immerse the ribbon in the solution for a few seconds, then remove it from the bowl and squeeze out the excess solution.

Many types of dye are available, including direct dye (available from art and craft suppliers) and fabric

dye pens. Ribbons may be coloured either when made up into a finished project or before needlework commences. This avoids the risk of a complex piece of work being ruined by inexperienced handling of dye stuffs. Pre-needlework dyeing is best carried out while the ribbon is still wet with permeation solution. Working on a protected surface, simply paint on the dye, allowing it to run to produce a subtle, graded effect or applying uniformly for an even colour change.

SIZEING RIBBONS

Sizeing prevents cut edges fraying, and adds body to ribbons. This is useful for flower making. If you plan to colour ribbons as well as size them, it is generally advisable to carry out the sizeing when the ribbons have dried out completely after dyeing. Starch and wallpaper paste are both options for sizeing fabric, but to recreate the projects in this book I recommend Fraycheck, or any other commercially available product especially designed for this purpose. As a rule, such products may be applied uniformly to the reverse of the ribbons, and allowed to dry before they are cut to shape, or applied with a cocktail stick to the cut edges of the ribbon shapes.

TRANSFERRING THE DESIGN

For some projects, a line drawing of the pattern is included. Some patterns and templates are actual size, and can be traced directly off the page. Where the patterns are too big for the book, they have been reduced in scale. Use a photocopier to enlarge them.

Always press the fabric so that it is smooth and even before you transfer a design. The quickest

method is to use dressmaker's carbon paper. Trace the design/template onto tracing paper. Cut a piece of fabric slightly larger than required and press flat. Mark horizontal and vertical lines through the centre of both the tracing paper design and the piece of fabric, using basting stitches to mark the fabric. Place the fabric right side up on a hard surface and the transfer paper shiny side down on the fabric.

Place the tracing paper design on top, matching the centre lines to the lines on the fabric. Pin the tracing paper and fabric together and trace over the design with pencil or ballpoint pen. Remove the transfer and tracing paper carefully. Extend the stitches slightly beyond the carbon lines so that they are not visible on the finished work. As dressmaker's carbon is ineffective on very textured fabrics, you will need to use an alternative for transferring a design onto fabrics such as velvet. To transfer a design by the running stitch method, trace the design onto tracing paper. Cut a piece of fabric slightly larger than required and press flat. Mark horizontal and vertical lines through the centre of both the tracing paper design and the piece of fabric, using basting stitches to mark the fabric. Place the tracing on the right side of the material, matching the centre lines, and pin in place. Using a coloured thread which will show clearly on the fabric, work running stitches through the layered paper and fabric, following the design carefully. Secure the beginnings and ends of each stitch line with back stitches. When the tracing is complete, lay the work on a flat surface and tear away the tracing paper. Remove the running stitches as the work is progressed.

STITCHES AND TECHNIQUES

Locking on

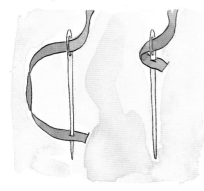

Buttonhole stitch

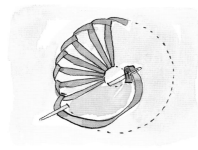

Buttonhole stitches are made in the same way as blanket stitches, except that here the stitches are placed as closely together as possible. This helps to form a firm edging. It is also possible to work buttonhole stitch in a circle, forming decorative spheres that look like flowers.

Buttonholed eyelets

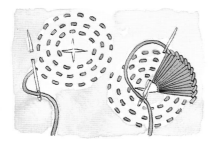

When a buttonholed circle is worked around a small hole cut in the fabric base, a buttonholed eyelet is formed. It can also be worked on small rings of plastic or metal. To strengthen the fabric to be covered by the eyelet, work rows of running stitch before working buttonhole stitch.

Feather stitch

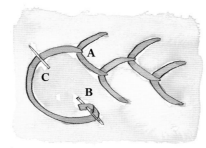

This is worked by bringing the needle through the fabric at A. Reinsert it at B, and come out again at C, catching the thread or ribbon under the needle before pulling it through. Repeat, alternating from side to side, along the stitch line.

French knots

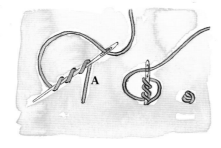

Useful for working flower stamens. Bring needle through the fabric at A. Holding thread or ribbon taut with one hand, wind it around around needle twice and reinsert needle near point A, keeping thread taut as you pull the needle through.

Long and short stitch

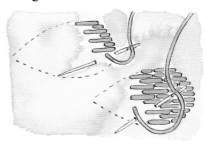

This is a filling stitch, worked similarly to satin stitch, but with stitches of varied lengths – producing a dynamic, broken texture, as on the bow of the ribbon-embroidered pelmet. To work this stitch, place straight stitches close together. The initial row of stitches should alternate between long and short, while the subsequent stitches should all be longer. Continue until the shape is filled.

Overcasting

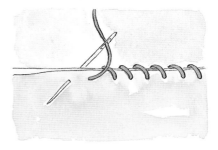

This is a technique that is frequently used to join pieces of fabric. Turn in the raw edges and hold them firmly together. Now work small, even stitches through both edges – working from right to left on the right side of the fabric. This stitch is also used as a decorative stitch, worked in either ribbon or thread. It has been used in various projects in the book, including the cushion trimmings and braided seat pad.

Satin stitch

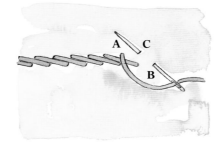

This consists of threads laid very close together, from one edge of a design to the other. Bring the needle through the fabric, from the wrong side to the right, at A. Reinsert the needle at B, and come out again at C, as close as possible to A. Repeat until the design is filled.

Slip stitch

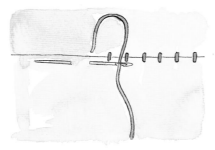

To produce a hemming stitch that is virtually invisible on the right side of the fabric, you need to do the following: first, fold the fabric under twice, and slide the needle through the folded edge. Then bring the needle out, pick up a single thread of the main fabric, and continue to stitch. The stitches should be spaced 3-6mm/⅛-¼in apart. Slip stitch is not a particularly strong stitch, although its invisibility makes it a very popular choice for hemming.

Stem stitch

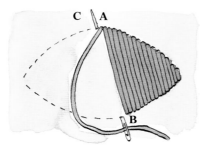

Good for outlining and making curving lines. It is is worked as for back-stitch, but the stitches overlap each other, diagonally, giving a rope-like effect. Bring the needle through the fabric, from the wrong side to the right, at A. Insert the needle at B, and come out again at C, half-way back along the stitch-line. Repeat, always keeping the thread to the same side of the needle.

Blanket stitch

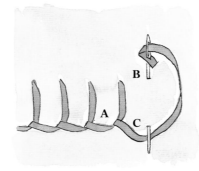

This stitch, often used to finish edges (especially on blankets), is also known as open buttonhole stitch. To work it, bring the needle through the fabric at A. Following the diagram above, insert the needle at B and come out again at C, catching the thread or ribbon under the needle before pulling it tight. The arms of the blanket stitch can be stitched in varying lengths for a decorative effect.

Bullion knots

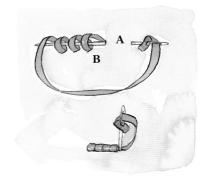

Bullion knots are similar to French knots, except that they create a larger stitch which is ideal for making flower centres, small leaves, ears of wheat etc. Bring the needle up through the fabric at A. Insert it at B, and bring it up again at A, leaving the needle in the fabric as shown. Wrap the ribbon flatly around the needle three or four times. Holding the ribbon wrapping firmly in place with one hand, pull the remaining ribbon

Back stitch

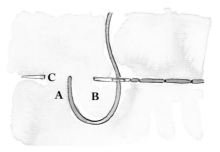

Used to make an outline, or a baseline for other decorative stitches. Bring the needle through the fabric, from the wrong side to the right, at A. Insert the needle at B, and come again at C. Insert the needle again at A. Proceed an equal distance further along the stitch line, past C. Repeat.

Lazy-daisy stitch

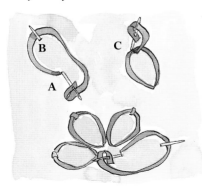

Variant of chain stitch. Bring needle up through fabric at A. Reinsert needle next to A, and bring through fabric again at B. Turn ribbon and slip beneath needle tip, taking care to keep ribbon flat. Hold loop down with thumb while pulling ribbon through, to close the loop. Reinsert needle at C to anchor the stitch.

Pistil stitch

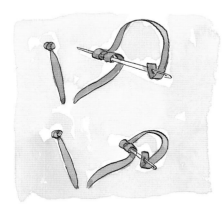

Pistil Stitch is also known as a long-tailed French knot. This is simply a French knot where the thread or ribbon extends from the knot to suggest a stalk. Work a French knot as usual, but instead of reinserting the needle close to the knot, reinsert it sufficiently far away to represent a stalk.

Running stitch

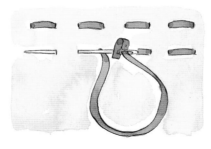

To work this fundamental stitch, you should pass the needle in and out of the fabric at regular intervals along the stitch line. If additional strength is what is required, work a back stitch every three stitches. This strengthened version of running stitch is called half-back stitch. When working this stitch in ribbon, take extra care to make the stitches even in size and tension. This is important as the width of the ribbon will magnify any discrepancies.

Straight stitch

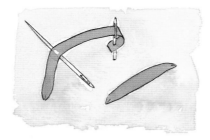

The fullness of ribbon means that even a simple straight stitch, when carefully worked, can represent a whole petal; while in thread embroidery many filling stitches would have to be worked to cover the same ground. As this stitch is such an important one in ribbon embroidery, it is worth taking the time to practise on spare fabric using different widths of ribbon, and experimenting with both allowing the ribbon to twist and keeping the ribbon flat, before embarking on a project.

Whipped running stitch

To work whipped running stitch in ribbon: Using a crewel needle, work a basic row of running stitch along the stitch line, making the stitches slightly longer than the width of ribbon used. It is important to keep the distance between the running stitches small and even. Bring the wrapping ribbon through the fabric from the back to the front, slightly to the right of the first running stitch, still using the crewel needle. You now need to change the needle to a tapestry needle so that the point does not pierce and shred the ribbons as you wrap. Using both hands on the surface of the work to manoeuvre the ribbon, pass the needle between the running stitches and the surface of the fabric, making sure that you keep the wrapping perfectly even. (Whipped running stitch – worked in ribbon – has been used on the shoe trees; see page 121.)

Furnishings

Curtains & tie-backs

Since the 16th century, machine- or hand-made netting has been embellished with stitches and applied tapes to simulate lace. Many examples were incredibly labour-intensive and finely wrought, but these delicate curtains use wide tapes simply gathered and appliquéd, to make a comparatively fast-growing design. A popular 19th-century pattern was the stitching together of several rows of tape in a chevron arrangement to make an insertion for bedding and other household linens. In this example, a single row of chevrons makes a pretty border. (See page 27.)

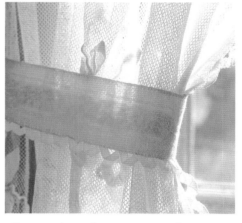

These curtains — which were originally part of a tablecloth or bedspread — were found languishing in a suitcase in an antiques shop. They employ another favoured 19th-century technique — that of running a stitch in a chevron pattern through linen tape, and drawing up the tape to create curved shapes such as the flower and leaf motifs. Both the folded chevron edging and the gathered motif methods are simple ways of adding interest to plain soft furnishings, and can be interpreted using a variety of ribbons. The matt simplicity of cotton and linen tapes adds sophistication to this overtly feminine treatment.

LEFT Cotton tapes on a fresh white ground mimic lace in a restrained manner.
ABOVE Simple chevrons of new cotton tape give a decorative flourish to tie-backs.

23

Tape curtains

ABILITY LEVEL
Intermediate

FINISHED SIZE
260 x 117cm/102½ x 46in
each curtain (including edging)

RIBBONS
120m/130yd of 6mm/¼in
cotton or linen tape

20m/21¾yd of 20mm/¾in
cotton or linen tape

6m/6½yd of 25mm/1in
cotton or linen tape

[NB. To calculate the amount
of tape or ribbon required for a
single chevron border, you need to
allow three times the linear
measurement.]

TOOLS
Crewel needle

Medium "Sharp" needle

FABRIC
Two pieces of cotton net,
each measuring 265cm x
118cm/104¼in x 46½in

OTHER MATERIALS
White stranded embroidery
cotton (six strands)

White cotton thread

White cotton cord for stems
(approx 40m/43½yd)

100 x 1cm/½in plastic or
metal eyelets

Decorative metal curtain clips

STITCHES AND TECHNIQUES
• Slip stitch
• Buttonhole stitch
• Ribbon flowers
• Ribbon leaves
• Transferring a design

MAKING UP
1 Fold in one of the long sides and
both the short ends of the net by
75mm/3in.

2 Apply the 6mm/¼in tape to
cover the raw edges. Pin in
place. Slipstitch through tape and
both of the layers of net to secure
the hems and cover the raw
edges. Press.

3 Apply 6mm/¼in tape along the
folded edges of the hems. Pin and
stitch in place.

4 Hand-stitch the 6mm/¼in
cotton tape to the perimeter tape
on the three neatened sides,
making sure that you fold evenly
into zig-zags as you stitch.

[See also instructions and illustration
on how to make the zig-zag
edging for the tie-back project –
step 3, page 27]

5 Transfer the design to the curtain.
(Template on page 25 shows a
quarter of the complete design.
Enlarge by 200%.)

6 Pin the straight lines of the
25mm/1in tape onto the net,
mitring at the corners and
turning under the raw ends.
Slipstitch in place.

7 Pin the 6mm/¼in cotton
tape in place to form the main
curved parts of the design.

Making the single leaves
8 Make the leaves using
the 20mm/¾in tape. For a
single leaf, cut a 5cm/2in length
of tape. Turn under each raw
end by 5mm/¼in. Fold one
neatened end into a point.
Pleat the other end of the tape
to form a leaf shape. Press.

Making the double leaves
9 To make the double leaves,
take a 10cm/4in length of
20mm/¾in tape. Turn under
each raw end by 5mm/¼in.
Fold each neatened end into
a point (as shown in the
illustration). At the centre of
the tape, make a pleat across
the width. Make a small tuck
across the pleat, to form a curve
where the leaves meet. Press.

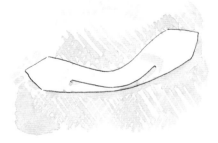

10 Stitch the double leaves in
place. Stitch the stems in place,
tucking the raw ends under the
narrow tape. Stitch the narrow
tape in place. Apply the single
leaves to cover the remaining raw
ends of the stems.

*RIGHT Enlarge this template to
200%. To make each curtain, "flip"
the design along the length so that
it is a mirror image.*

Making the flowers

11 To make the flowers, take a 30.5cm/12in length of the 20mm/¾in wide tape. Join the raw ends using a 5mm/¼in seam allowance. Stitch a chevron pattern of running stitch along the length as in the diagram. Pull up tightly into a flower shape. Press.

12 Slipstitch the flowers onto the netting.

Making the eyelets

13 For the eyelets, you should work buttonhole stitch (see page 18 in the *Before you begin* section) in stranded embroidery cotton tightly around each rigid ring. Slipstitch in place.

14 Turn in the remaining long, raw edge of the curtain by 6mm/¼in, toward the right side of the design. Cover the raw edge using the 6mm/¼in tape.

15 Finally, attach the clips to your curtains.

ADAPTING TO FIT THE SIZE OF YOUR WINDOWS

It would be relatively simple to adapt this pattern to make curtains of different sizes to fit your windows.

When transferring the design from the book, you need to extend or reduce the straight lines of the pattern as appropriate. Base any change in scale around the long, straight runs of tape as indicated on the artwork.

It is important to re-draw the twists and curves so that they are placed centrally along the straight lines, following the original design on the previous page.

USING DIFFERENT FABRICS

This curtain design would also work on other semi-sheer fabrics – voile being a good example.

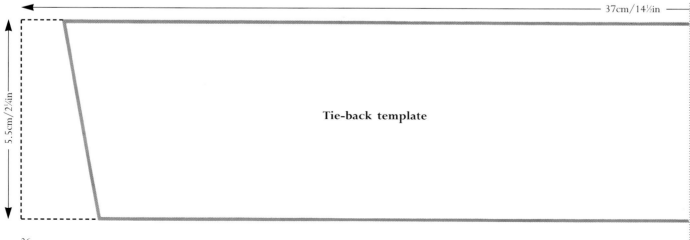

37cm/14½in

5.5cm/2¼in

Tie-back template

White tie-backs

ABILITY LEVEL
Beginner

FINISHED SIZE
35 x 6.5cm/14 x 2½in

RIBBONS
Each tie-back
requires:

37 x 5.5cm/14½ x 2¼in
cotton braid

75cm x 6mm/29½ x ¼in
cotton tape

TOOLS
Medium "Sharp" needle

FABRICS
None

OTHER MATERIALS
White cotton thread

4 brass rings, 2.5cm/1in

STITCHES AND TECHNIQUES
• Slip stitch
• Overcasting

MAKING UP
1 Mark 1cm/½in in from each
end along the bottom edge
of the braid. Cut from each
corner of the top edge, to each
mark, forming sloped ends as
on the template shown on
this page.

2 To neaten each raw, sloping
end, fold over 5mm/¼in twice,
forming a double hem. Slipstitch,
neatly tucking in the excess raw
material at the top.

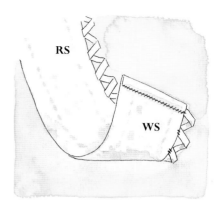

3 Hand-stitch the narrow cotton
tape in place along the lower
edge of the braid, folding evenly
into zig-zags as you stitch. Conceal
the ends of the tape within the hems
at each end of the braid; fix with a
few stitches.

4 Securely hand-stitch brass rings
onto the top corners of the braid.

Floral pelmet

Ribbon embroidery of the 19th century is often not immediately recognisable as such. The colouring is extremely delicate, so it is possible for the casual viewer to incorrectly identify the stitches as being worked in carefully shaded embroidered threads. This glorious Rococo pelmet – with its rich gold bullion trim – is a wonderful example of how wide ribbons, if delicately shaded, can capture a design in very few stitches, creating great depth and charm. Looking closely at the pelmet, the actual stitching is quite ungainly – yet again demonstrating the highly forgiving nature of ribbon embroidery.

Some of the ribbons here are ombré – where the shading has been woven into the ribbon across the width. Other ribbons, such as the sprays of lilac flowers and scattered forget-me-nots, have been hand-tinted by the embroiderer with watercolour or dye, after they had been stitched in place. Ribbons were often painted to add definition; an inventive skill which deserves a revival. It is probable that the ribbons were originally much more vividly coloured, but to recreate the subtlety of this design, understatement is recommended. Over the following pages you will find a template of half of the pelmet design. Note that the bow on page 33 straddles the middle of the design.

RIGHT AND ABOVE A simple calico door dressing is given a flamboyant finish with this gold bullion-fringed, ribbon-embroidered pelmet on gleaming satin. Some of the ribbons are ombré while others have been hand-tinted.

COLOUR KEY

Thread/ribbon type/stitch

- DMC 445/Anchor 288; Fr.knot
- 13mm citrus ombré silk ribbon
- 13mm green ombré silk ribbon
- 13mm yellow ombré ribbon
- DMC 3363/Anchor 262; bullion
- DMC989/Anchor 41; satin/stem
- Pink ombré silk ribbon
- White ribbon coloured lilac
- White ribbon coloured blue
- DMC B5200/Anchor 1; l/short.

ABILITY LEVEL

Intermediate

FINISHED SIZE

186 x 25cm/73 x 10in
(excluding fringe)

RIBBONS

25m/27yd of white 7mm/¼in silk

22m/24yd of green ombré
13mm/½in silk

1.5m/1½yd of golden yellow
ombré 13mm/½in silk

1m/1yd of pink ombré silk
13mm/½in

1m/1yd pink ombré 7mm/¼in silk

8m/9yd of citrus green ombré
13mm/½in silk

TOOLS

Medium "Sharp" needle for fine
silk thread

Crewel needle for ribbon
embroidery

FABRIC

1 piece of white or ivory satin 189 x
28cm/74½ x 11½in

1 piece of white or ivory furnishing
cotton 189cm x 35cm/74½ x 11½in

OTHER MATERIALS

Pale green stranded embroidery cotton (DMC 989/Anchor 241)

Dark green stranded embroidery cotton (DMC 3363/Anchor 262)

Yellow stranded embroidery cotton (DMC 445/Anchor 288)

White stranded embroidery cotton (DMC B5200/Anchor 1)

1 x 189cm/74½in length of 8cm/3in deep gold bullion fringe

13 x 1.5cm/¾in diameter brass rings

White silk thread

Pale green silk thread

Pale blue and lilac fabric dyes, dye pens or watercolours and small brush (optional)

STITCHES AND TECHNIQUES
- Sewing with ribbon
- French knots
- Bullion stitch
- Stem stitch
- Satin stitch
- Long and short stitch
- Straight stitch
- Slip stitch
- Dyeing and painting ribbons

MAKING UP

1 Press the satin so that it is square and even.

2 Transfer the design. The template provided here should be enlarged by 130%. Note that the main pattern at repeats at the point where the bow on page 33 is straddling the centre. To complete the design as shown on the photograph, "flip" it so that the second half is a mirror image of the template provided.

3 Embroider the central bow motif in long and short stitch (using Anchor 288/DMC 445) and stems (Anchor 241/DMC 989) and tiny

leaves (dark leaves DMC 3363/ Anchor 262, pale leaves DMC 954/Anchor 989) in stem stitch and satin stitch respectively, using embroidery thread.

4 Embroider the leaves and flowers in ribbon, being careful to control the twists and folds to produce a result similar to the illustration. When the pattern requires that an extensive length of ribbon remains flat on the surface, for example, as in the long smooth leaves, secure the ribbon intermittently with tiny stab stitches in toning silk thread.

5 Paint dye or watercolour shading onto the ribbon-embroidered lilac and forget-me-nots. (This is optional.)

6 Using embroidery cotton, stitch the flower centres in French knots (see page 17 in the *Before You Begin* section) and bullion stitch (for the large orange-coloured flowers).

7 Leaving a 1.5cm/½in seam allowance, hand- or machine-stitch the finished embroidery to the cotton fabric, with the right sides facing. Make sure that you

leave a small gap for turning. Turn right side out and slipstitch closed.

8 Hand-stitch the bullion fringe in slip stitch along the bottom edge of the completed pelmet, turning in neatly at the ends.

9 Using silk thread, stitch the brass rings in place (using buttonhole stitch), evenly spaced just below the top edge of the reverse of the pelmet.

Log cabin throw

Ribbons are perfect for constructing log cabin quilts. The need for painstakingly accurate cutting of narrow strips is removed, leaving only the ends to be trimmed after stitching each ribbon in place. A complex effect is achieved with minimal effort.

This unusual Art Deco example, a blaze of vivid satins and grosgrains, was a very lucky find. I actually came upon it while on a trip to find traditional blankets in rural Wales. In a simply furnished, predominantly white-painted interior, this dazzling quilt literally illuminated the whole of one room. On close inspection, the quilt reveals even more inventiveness in its design than is immediately visible. Several slightly different textures have been used within each colour grouping. The black alone features jacquard satin, plain satin, grosgrain and velvet; and occasionally, joined strips are found within a single "log". This apparently random patterning probably occurred because the maker ran out of a particular texture during stitching, but even these seemingly unplanned variations have been carefully placed. Each quarter is an exact mirror of its three neighbours in the design. I have included details of these deliberate variations so that a similarly pleasing textural result can be achieved.

The inclusion of appropriate odds and ends from your workbasket will further enhance the traditionally parsimonious nature of this project. The original quilt uses both ribbons and fabric scraps; including even the bright selvedge stripes that are usually discarded. The differing textures of the ribbons throw the design into subtle relief, even with such minimal quilting as the ties at the intersection of each block.

RIGHT Startlingly bright red ribbons in red, oyster and gold achieve stained glass clarity against a rich black backing worked in a gloriously tactile mixture of velvet, grosgrain, jacquard and satin.

ABILITY LEVEL Intermediate

FINISHED SIZE 165cm/65in square

RIBBONS

4m/4½yd of 2.5cm/1in woven-edge oyster satin

20m/21¾yd of 2.5cm/1in woven-edge red satin

16m/17½yd of 2.5cm/1in woven-edge mustard satin

8m/8¾yd of 2.5cm/1in mustard grosgrain

12m/13yd of 2.5cm/1in woven-edge russet jacquard

12m/13yd of 2.5cm/1in russet woven-edge shot

16m/17½yd of 2.5cm/1in orange grosgrain

12m/13yd of 2.5cm/1in purple woven edge satin

68m/73¾yd of 2.5cm/1in black grosgrain

24m/26yd of 2.5cm/1in black woven-edge satin

8m/8¾yd of 2.5cm/1in black jacquard woven-edge satin

5.5m/6yd of 5.5cm/2¼in black velvet woven-edge for log cabin centres

TOOLS

Quilting pins

Quilting needle

Chenille needle

FABRIC

Medium-weight "Homespun" cotton, to make 100 foundation pieces, each 18.5cm/7⅜in square.

Heavy-weight buff-coloured cotton to make a backing 168cm/66¼in square

Heavy-weight buff-coloured cotton measuring 165cm/65in x approximately 10cm/4in (to make a sleeve if you wish to hang the finished quilt)

NB. The exact depth of this piece of fabric is dependent upon the circumference of pole you are using to suspend the quilt.

[see also page 38** if you are hand-stitching the quilt together]

Black satin, sufficient to make 7m/7¾yd of 5cm/2in wide bias-cut strips to cover the piping cord.

OTHER MATERIALS

Coton Perlé (pearlized cotton) embroidery thread to be used for the ties.

7m/7¾yd of 6mm/¼in piping cord

Polyester thread for stitching ribbons

Wooden pole (if you wish to hang the quilt)

2 cup hooks (if you wish to hang the quilt)

STITCHES AND TECHNIQUES
• Machine-stitching or back stitching

MAKING UP

1 Using a pencil and ruler, draw diagonal lines from corner to corner across a foundation piece. This will help you to mark the centre.

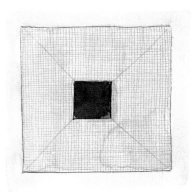

2 Cut a 5.5cm/2¼in length of the black velvet ribbon to form the central square. Baste it face up, to the middle of the foundation pieces.

3 Position a length of the black satin ribbon right sides facing along right-hand woven-edge of central velvet square. Stitch through three layers leaving a 5mm/³⁄₁₆in seam allowance along woven edges of ribbons.

4 Trim ribbon to length and press flat.

5 Turn the work clockwise. Position another length of the black satin ribbon – with right sides facing – along the right-hand edge of the newly created patch. Stitch in place, making sure that you leave a 5mm/³⁄₁₆in seam allowance as before. Trim the satin ribbon to length. Press flat, right sides face up.

6 Turn the work clockwise. Position a length of the oyster satin ribbon right sides facing, along the right-hand edge of the patch. Stitch in place as before. Trim the ribbon to length. Press flat, right sides face up.

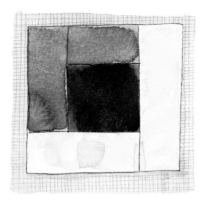

7 Now turn the work clockwise again. Take another length of the oyster satin ribbon; put in position and stitch in place. Trim and press, as before.

8 Continue in this way, adding ribbon strips by following the piecing diagram to make a completed block.

9 Make the remaining 99 blocks following steps 1 to 8 using the appropriate ribbons, following the assembly list and colour map.

Assembly list
Number of blocks of each configuration required (total: 100)

Oyster satin & black grosgrain 4
Red satin & black satin 4
Red satin & black grosgrain 16
Mustard satin and black grosgrain 8
Mustard satin and black satin 8
Mustard grosgrain & black grosgrain 8
Russet shot satin & black grosgrain 12
Russet jacquard & black satin jacquard 8
Russet jacquard & black grosgrain 4
Orange & black grosgrain 16
Purple satin & black satin 12

10 Piece the blocks together as follows, using the assembly diagram as a guide to exact placement of colours and textures:

Place one finished block on top of its neighbouring block, right sides facing, matching the edges. Make sure that the blocks are placed in the correct arrangement of light and shade. Pin, baste and stitch together. Use a 1.5cm/⅝in seam allowance throughout the whole piecing process.

11 Press the seam open. Following the colour diagrams, make five rows of five blocks for each quarter of the quilt.

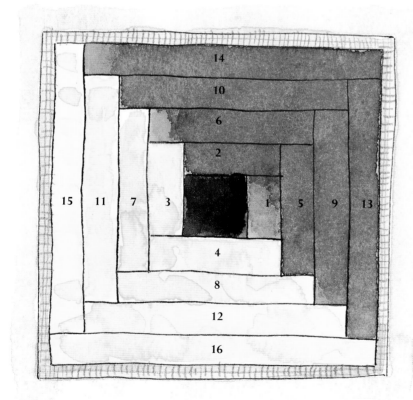

Piecing diagram

12 Pin, baste and stitch each row of five blocks together, right sides facing, following the diagram.

13 Press the seams open. When you have pieced together each quarter of the quilt (consisting of five rows of five columns), pin, baste, and stitch the quarters together, right sides facing, following the diagram. Each quarter is simply a mirror image of its neighbour.

14 Press the seams open.

The piping

15 For the piping, cut strips 5cm/2in wide, on the bias of the black satin. Join the short ends, right sides facing, leaving a 1.5cm/⅝in seam allowance, and press seams open. Continue joining pieces in this way until you have a 7m/7¾yd length of bias binding. Place the piping cord lengthways along the centre of the wrong side of the bias strip. Fold the strip over to encapsulate the cord. Sew close to the cord, using a zipper foot if machine-stitching.

16 Pin the piping to the right side of the pieced top, aligning the raw edges. Snip the seam allowance at the corners to facilitate smooth turning. Baste in place at the seam line, 1.5cm/ ⅝in from the raw edges. Stitch in place.

17 Make a second line of stitching 6mm/¼in toward the raw edge, for additional strength. Fold the raw edges toward the back of the pieced top and press in place.

18 Prepare the backing by joining pieces as necessary to make a 168cm/66¼in square. Around the edge of the square, turn a 1.5cm/⅝in seam allowance toward the wrong side of the fabric, either mitring or making straight folds at the corners. Press flat.

19 Slipstitch the backing fabric to the pieced top, concealing the stitches within the seam line of the piping.

20 Tie the quilt layers together at the intersection of each block. For each tie, thread a chenille needle with two complementary colours of Coton Perlé. Starting from the rear of the quilt, take the needle through all the layers, leaving an end about 3cm/1¼in long. Catch only the seam allowance of the pieced top so that the tie fixes, but does not show on the surface of the quilt. Bring the needle back to the rear of the quilt close to the original entry hole. Take the needle down through the layers, then up again in the same way. Remove the needle, tie off the loose ends in a reef knot and trim to 2.5cm/1in.

PREPARING THE QUILT FOR DISPLAY

To display the quilt as a hanging it is necessary for you to purchase a sturdy wooden pole, approximately the width of a broom handle, and two correspondingly sized cup hooks.

1 Take the piece of heavy-weight buff-coloured cotton 165cm/65in x approx 10cm/4in. Press so that it is square and even.

2 Turn under the short edges toward the wrong side of the fabric twice. (Include seam allowance of 1.5cm/½in.) Pin, baste and hem each neatly. Press.

3 Pin one long edge of the fabric close to one edge of the quilt – on the reverse – taking care to pin through the backing fabric only.

4 Flap the fabric right side out and place the pole underneath it to ascertain the exact location of the remaining seam. Be sure to check, when the pole is taking the strain of the fabric, that the sleeve will not be visible above the edge of the quilt.

5 When you are satisfied with the position of the sleeve, backstitch the top seam securely and slipstitch the bottom seam.

** You may like to make an identical sleeve for the opposite side of the quilt, so that it can be turned occasionally. Turning a wall-hung quilt will place less strain on the stitches holding the pieces together. This is particularly important if a quilt has been hand-stitched, rather than machine-sewn, as machine-sewn seams are generally much stronger.

KEY

G Grosgrain
S Satin
SS Shot Satin
J Jacquard
SJ Satin Jacquard

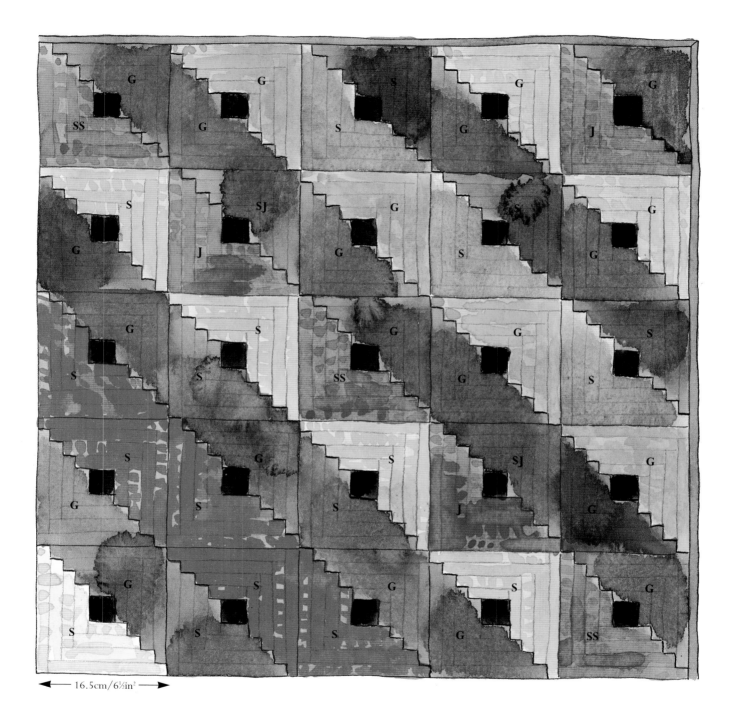

16.5cm/6½in²

Violet tablecloth

The colours of this pretty tablecloth have not faded with time. The deep purple and yellow-green ribbons remain very vivid, and are perfectly complemented by the citrus bright satin backing. The cloth was kindly loaned by a friend who has an amazing ribbon shop. Her zestful, outgoing personality and infectious passion for ribbons are perfectly reflected in this exuberant piece.

This is a particularly good project for a beginner to tackle. The tablecloth is composed of only a few basic embroidery stitches and is sewn using wide ribbons – so the result will be bold and fast-growing. Simple straight stitches in 13mm/½in-ribbon, for the flowers, border and most of the leaves, produce a wonderful three-dimensional look with minimal effort. Ombré ribbons have been added for a subtle, shaded effect. A wide range of stitches have been used on the tablecloth, making it an interesting project to undertake.

Random-dyed ribbons (see dyeing/painting ribbons on page 16 of the *Before You Begin* section) would make a contemporary alternative, or you could try painting your own ribbons with dye for a traditional result.

Embroidering with wide ribbons is perfect for what might otherwise be extremely time-consuming projects, such as bordering curtains and bedlinens.

RIGHT Crisp apple-green and deep violet silk ribbons are an unexpectedly successful combination against the neutrality of well-laundered natural linen. Simple straight stitches produce a bold design gratifyingly quickly.

ABILITY LEVEL
Beginner

FINISHED SIZE
86.5 x 86.5cm/34 x 34in

RIBBONS
Approximately 24m/26yd
each of:

Dark purple silk 13mm/½in or
7mm/¼in*

Lilac silk 13mm/½in or
7mm/¼in*

Pale lilac silk 13mm/½in or
7mm/¼in*

Yellow-green silk 13mm/½in or
7mm/¼in*

Approximately 8m/8¾yd
each of:

Dark green ombré or random-dyed
silk 4mm/³⁄₁₆in

Pale green ombré or random-dyed
silk 4mm/³⁄₁₆in

* see note on page 45

TOOLS
Chenille needle
(for ribbon embroidery)

Crewel needle
(for thread embroidery)

Embroidery hoop (optional)

FABRIC
One piece of natural linen
88.5 x 88.5cm/35 x 35in

One piece of yellow-green satin
88 x 88cm/34¼ x 34¼in

OTHER MATERIALS
Pale green embroidery cotton
(DMC 2369/Anchor 214)

Yellow embroidery cotton
(DMC 2745/Anchor 292)

Polyester cotton thread to match
the satin

STITCHES AND TECHNIQUES
- Slip stitch
- Feather stitch
- Stem stitch
- French knots
- Straight stitch
- Ombré dyeing
- Sewing with ribbon
- Transferring designs

MAKING UP
1 Press the linen so that it is square
and even.

2 Transfer the design onto the
linen, using the plan on page 42
and the pattern templates on the
following pages. You need to
enlarge the designs by 140%.

3 Stitch the stems in stem stitch
using the green embroidery cotton
(DMC 2369/Anchor 214).

4 Embroider the ribbon flowers
in straight stitch.

5 Embroider the ribbon leaves in
straight stitch.

6 Embroider the ribbon border in
feather stitch.

7 Stitch the French knots using the
yellow embroidery cotton.

8 If the finished embroidery
needs pressing, you should

do this on the reverse of the
work, using very light pressure.
Press the piece on a well-padded
surface – for example, a folded
towel covered with a clean
white cloth. You should take
particular care to avoid flattening
the ribbon stitches.

9 Fold under 5mm/¼in twice
along each edge of the linen to
make a double hem, folding at
the corners. Press, pin and baste
in place.

10 Fold under 1cm/⅜in along each
side of the satin. Press. Pin, then
slipstitch neatly to the reverse of
the tablecloth.

MATCHING THE ORIGINAL
If you look closely at the
original embroidery on the
violet tablecloth, it is clear that
one of the golden rules of ribbon
embroidery has been flouted.
The flowers, and some of the
leaves, have been stitched using
a needle that was not large enough
to pierce an adequately sized hole
through the ground fabric.
As the wide ribbon was forced
through the small hole, it did
not have sufficient space to
spread evenly, and subsequently
became creased and folded.
    The result is that, although wide
ribbon has been used, the finished
petals look only half as wide as
the ribbon used. It is possible
that this was the desired effect,
although it seems very unlikely
given that the ombré-embroidered
leaves have been stitched using
an appropriately sized needle,
which means that the stitches sit
comfortably at full spread on the
surface fabric.

For that reason, specifications have been included here for embroidering the flowers and some of the leaves in either narrow or wide ribbon.

To achieve an effect identical to the original, buy ribbons (measuring 13mm/½in) and a needle that makes a hole slightly too small for the ribbon to pass through smoothly. [If I was stitching the project myself, I would use 7mm/¼in-wide ribbon, and a correctly sized needle. This would be more economical than buying expensive, wider silk ribbon. It would also give a more delicate result, since the flowers will not be of a doubled thickness of ribbon.]

ALTERNATIVES

This design would make a pretty border on plain curtains. Choose neutral shades of ribbon in taupe, beige, white and stone, worked in calico or linen for a clean, contemporary look.

COLOUR KEY

Thread/ribbon type/stitch

- DMC 2745/Anchor 292; F.knot
- 4mm/³⁄₁₆in ombré dyed ribbon
- Ombré silk ribbon
- 13mm/½in or 7mm/¼in ribbon
- DMC 2369/Anchor 214; stem
- 4mm/³⁄₁₆in ombré ribbon
- 13mm/½in or 7mm/¼in silk ribb.
- 13mm/½in or 7mm/¼in silk ribb.

Bedding

Rosebud cot quilt

Made for my daughter's first birthday, this romantic quilt revives the tradition of making luxurious silk quilts for special occasions – including weddings and christenings, where they would be placed on the bed as part of the display of gifts.

The design on this rare and delicate quilt is based on 19th-century English log cabin quilts, which were made of wide silk hat ribbons. This ingenious method produces an heirloom-quality hand-stitched quilt in just a couple of evenings. The woven selvedges of the ribbons obviate the need for tedious hemming and turning. The ribbons are applied directly to the quilt lining and backing, so what is normally a two-stage process of piecing and quilting is worked simultaneously; because of the width of the ribbons, only a few lines of stitching are required. The traditional log cabin pattern has been adapted slightly to produce a rectangular quilt which fits a standard cot mattress, rather than the traditional square.

I found the breathtakingly pretty original Victorian silk hat ribbon tucked away in a dark corner of an antique shop. Many old ribbons have become unusably brittle with time, but this length, stored away from sunlight and damp, has retained its original flexibility. The deliciously fine and crisp silk is as translucent and fragile as a watercolour; a more robust everyday quilt may be made from contemporary cotton or satin ribbons. A cool silk quilt is a delight-ful and practical gift for a summer baby. For a winter gift, you could add more layers of natural interlining (wool, silk wadding or cotton bump), or substitute natural wadding – available from specialist quilting suppliers. NB: The pillow pictured was for display purposes only. Pillows are not recommended for babies of any age.

RIGHT This quilt, produced for a special occasion from antique silk ribbons, may be constructed from contemporary ribbons for a more resilient finish.

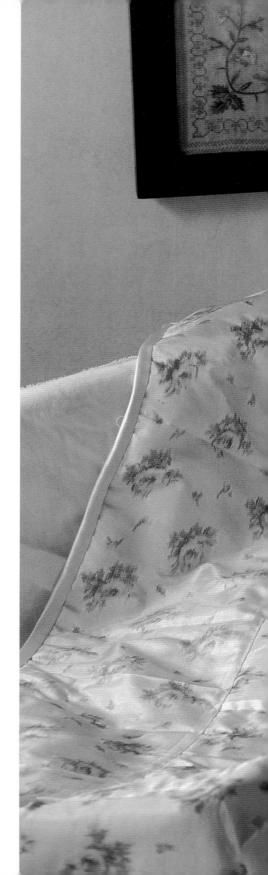

ABILITY LEVEL Beginner

FINISHED SIZE
71 x 99cm/28 x 39in

RIBBONS
5.25m/5½yd of 15cm/6in woven-edge silk millinery ribbon

TOOLS
Fine quilting needle & quilting pins

FABRIC
1 piece of natural interlining
71 x 99cm/28 x 39in

1 piece of pre-shrunk, first-quality calico 71 x 99cm/28 x 39in

OTHER MATERIALS
4m/4½yd white satin bias binding

White silk thread

Pencil or fade-out fabric marker

STITCHES AND TECHNIQUES
• Running stitch
• Mitring
• Attaching bias binding

MAKING UP
1 Press all the materials so that they are square and even. Place interlining on top of calico.

2 Using a pencil or fade-out fabric marker mark interlining diagonally from corner to corner to find the centre (above left). Working from the centre outward, baste the two layers together, along the marked lines. Pin a 15cm/6in length of ribbon centrally across interlining, with raw ends facing the long sides. (See "map" of finished quilt for correct direction of the pattern.) Baste in place and remove the pins.

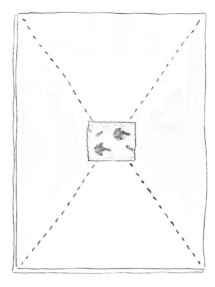

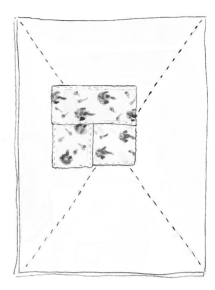

3 Pin and baste a 15cm/6in length of ribbon across one end of the first length of ribbon, covering raw edge by 1cm/½in.

4 Pin and baste a 29cm/11½in length of ribbon across the two basted pieces of ribbon, covering raw end of ribbon applied in step 3, and selvedge of the ribbon applied in step 2 by 1cm/½in (see above right.)

5 Pin and baste a 29cm/11½in length of ribbon across the ends of the ribbons applied in steps 2 and 4, covering the raw ends by 1cm/½in.

6 Pin and baste a 43cm/17in length of ribbon across ends of ribbons attached in steps 3 and 5, covering raw ends/selvedge of first ribbon applied in step 2, by 1cm/½in.

7 Pin and baste ribbon (43cm/17in) alongside that applied in step 6, covering selvedge by 1cm/½in.

8 Pin and baste ribbon (43cm/17in) alongside that applied in step 7, covering selvedge by 1cm/½in.

9 Pin and baste a 43cm/17in length of ribbon alongside the ribbon attached in step 4, covering the selvedge, and also covering the remaining raw end of the ribbon applied in step 5 by 1cm/½in.

10 Pin and baste a 43cm/17in length of ribbon alongside the ribbon applied in step 9, covering the selvedge by 1cm/½in.

11 Pin and baste a 99cm/39in length of ribbon to cover all ribbon edges along left-hand side of the quilt by 1cm/½in. Pin and baste a 99cm/39in length of ribbon to cover all ribbon edges along right-hand side of quilt by 1cm/½in – completely covering the interlining with ribbon strips.

12 Working from the middle outward, stitch through all of the layers of the quilt, close to the woven edges of each of the ribbons, using a small running stitch in silk thread. Then stitch bias binding in place around the perimeter of the quilt, mitring or folding square at the corners.

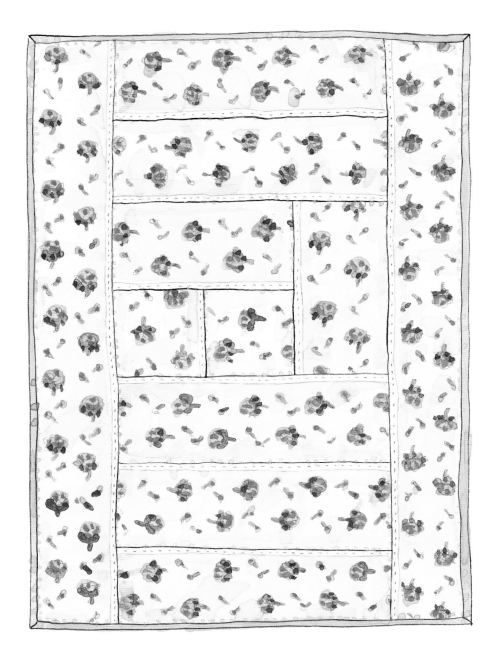

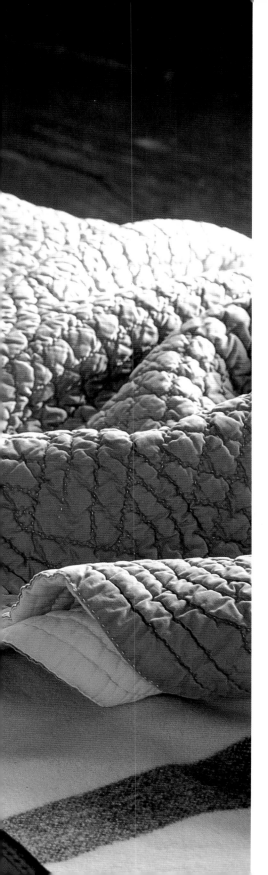

Blanket trimmings

Traditional woollen blankets seem to be very popular once again, having been temporarily ousted by a preference for duvets. These deeply covetable Welsh blankets have been passed down from generation to generation. Some date from the late 18th century. These early examples were woven on narrow looms and then stitched together to make a full blanket. On close inspection, the hand-stitched central seam is just visible.

Originally, the blankets were finished at each raw end with either blanket stitch or a knotted fringe. However, regular use over the course of many years has taken its toll. As blankets wore out — particularly as the weaker ends were tugged at by generations of over enthusiastic children — woollen braids were added to strengthen the frayed edges. Traditionally, these were simple woollen tapes in the same natural colours as the blankets; the charcoal gray of the local sheep's wool, and the deep red of the madder root.

The ruched frill trim, ribbon blanket stitch, and shiny rayon tape are all included here as contemporary versions of traditional techniques, employed chiefly for their decorative virtues.

Decorated blankets are useful in the living room as well as the bedroom. Throw them over an old sofa for a quick disguise when unexpected guests call, or snuggle up in comfort when the winter weather does its work.

Charity shops are a good source of natural wool blankets. They are often not displayed because their bulk occupies too much space, so ask for details of what is in the stockroom. It is important, however, to always check for moth damage before purchasing.

LEFT Rich madder reds, charcoal grays and natural creamy wool provide a traditional colour scheme for an inviting array of ribbon-trimmed blankets.

RIBBON-TRIMMED BEDLINEN

Following the basic techniques described over the following pages it is possible to enhance all kinds of bedlinen and household articles at very little expense, and with reasonably minimal effort. Just a small amount of ribbon appliquéd to a blanket will add to its appeal. When appliquéing ribbon, simply make sure that you always stitch each woven-edge of the ribbon in the same direction, to avoid unsightly puckering. A twin-needle attachment on a sewing machine makes light work of attaching narrow ribbons in this way.

Another simple idea is to add monograms using lengths of narrow ribbon gathered up and stitched to the ground fabric in letter forms. This can be particularly effective.

Although most people think of traditional blankets as being edged with wide satin ribbon, this is in fact a comparatively recent innovation – and, as such, has not been included in the selection of traditional blanket edgings.

Until recently, manufacturers produced good-quality, wide, bias-cut satin ribbons that were designed to give a new lease of life to worn blanket edges. Sadly, such ribbons have largely been discontinued, as contemporary tastes in bedlinen have turned toward duvets.

As these ribbons are no longer generally available, I considered that it was best to omit this from the selection of contemporary edgings (see page 56). However, since I am frequently asked how to recreate this charming effect, I have included instructions here on how to make your own satin ribbon edging.

MAKING HOME-MADE SATIN RIBBON EDGING

The word ribbon simply means "a narrow strip", and some ribbons today are still literally narrow strips cut from a wider strip of cloth, rather than being woven as purpose-designed narrow strips with two selvedges, so this home-made edging is as authentic and traditional a ribbon as any that may be purchased. Obviously, the long edges are not woven, but as these are contained within the seams, this does not present a problem.

If you are making a small blanket suitable for a baby or a doll, a pleasing result can be achieved by scaling down the width of the satin strips slightly to suit the size of your own ribbon binding as opposed to using ready-made. Also, you can make satin binding that is exactly the required shade, rather than compromising within a limited palette of purchased edgings.

For very subtle results, choose satin that almost exactly matches the colour of the blanket. Although dramatic effects can be achieved using highly contrasting shades, this does not produce such a glamorous effect.

1 Measure the length of the edge that you wish to bind, and add 5cm/2in for turning at each end.

2 Purchase best-quality slipper satin to the appropriate length, rather than across the width of the satin, so that there are no joins in the finished edging. You could also cut the strip on the bias, although if you are using dress satin – and making anything larger than a baby's blanket – this will almost certainly necessitate joining strips together to achieve the required length.

3 Cut each strip required to the appropriate length, plus an additional amount for the seam allowance, and 12.5cm/5in wide.

4 Fold under 1.5cm/½in along each long edge of each strip, toward the reverse of the fabric. Press to secure.

5 Pin, baste and machine-stitch the strip in place 5cm/2in from the edge you wish to trim, right sides facing, so that the binding will encapsulate the edge when turned around it and slip-stitched in place.

[Note that this measurement will change if you have scaled down the width of the strip to suit a smaller blanket. To calculate this, simply halve the width of the strip, allow 1.5cm/½in seam allowance, then stitch at this distance from the edge.]

6 Turn in the first raw end. Slipstitch in place.

7 Bring the binding around to encompass the blanket edge. Pin and slipstitch in place.

8 Slipstitch the remaining raw end closed.

Traditional blankets-1

[Madder tape on single side of blanket]

ABILITY LEVEL
Beginner

FINISHED SIZE
Individual to each blanket

RIBBONS
Madder-coloured wool military braid the length of blanket to be trimmed, plus 3cm/1in for turning under the raw ends

TOOLS
Medium "Sharp" needle

FABRIC
Natural wool blanket

OTHER MATERIALS
Thread to match tape and thread to match blanket

APPLYING THE RIBBON
1 Cut off any existing worn edges from the blanket. Turn under 1.5cm/½in twice and press flat. Pin, baste and hand- or machine-stitch the new hem in place.

2 Pin, baste and slipstitch tape along the top side of the blanket, turning under raw ends of tape neatly.

Traditional blankets-2

[Black military tape on both sides of blanket]

ABILITY LEVEL   Beginner

FINISHED SIZE
Individual to each blanket

RIBBONS
Black wool military braid 3.5cm/1¼in wide twice the length of blanket to be trimmed, plus 6cm/12½in for turning under the raw ends

OR   Black wool military braid 7cm/2¾in wide x the length of blanket to be trimmed plus 3cm/1¼in for turning under the raw ends

TOOLS
Medium "Sharp" needle

FABRIC
Natural wool blanket

OTHER MATERIALS
Thread to match tape

APPLYING THE RIBBON
1 Cut off the worn edges of the blanket.

[NB. If the edges are in a reasonable condition the tape may simply be stitched in place to cover the existing edges.]

2 If using the 3.5cm/1¼in wide tape, pin, baste and slipstitch the tape 3.5cm/1¼in from the edge of the blanket along both sides, turning under the raw ends of the tape neatly.

3 Slipstitch the two pieces of tape together, encapsulating the blanket edge between the two.

Alternatively: You could use a double width tape and fold in half to encapsulate the blanket edge, tucking in the raw end of the tape neatly. Pin, baste and slipstitch in place.

Traditional blankets-3

[Jacquard-woven ribbon on single side of blanket]

ABILITY LEVEL
Beginner

FINISHED SIZE
Individual to each blanket

RIBBONS
Madder-coloured jacquard-woven ribbon approximately 7.5cm/3in wide x the length of blanket to be trimmed plus cm/1in for turning under the raw ends

TOOLS
Medium "Sharp" needle

FABRIC
Natural wool blanket

OTHER MATERIALS
Thread to match tape

Thread to match blanket

APPLYING THE RIBBON
1 Cut off any worn edges on the blanket. Turn under 1.5cm/½in twice and press flat. Then, pin, baste and hand- or machine-stitch the new hem in place.

2 Pin, baste and slipstitch the tape along the top side of the blanket, turning under the raw ends of the tape neatly.

Alternatively: you could encapsulate the blanket edge fully within the braid by folding it in half lengthways; or apply the braid to both sides and overcast the top edges together.

Contemporary blankets-1

[Ribbon blanket stitch]

ABILITY LEVEL
Beginner

FINISHED SIZE
Individual to each blanket

RIBBONS
Narrow woven-edge double-face satin ribbon. e.g. 2mm/⅟₁₆in brown ribbon used here; approximately 4 times the length of blanket to be trimmed

TOOLS
Crewel needle

FABRIC
Natural wool blanket

APPLYING THE RIBBON
1 Cut off any existing worn edges on the blanket. Turn under 1.5cm/½in twice and press flat. Pin and baste in place.

2 Stitch blanket stitch along the turned edge, using the ribbon in place of thread.

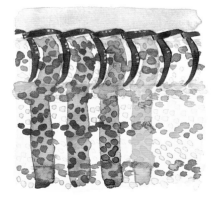

Contemporary blankets-2

[Chevron-gathered ribbon ruffle trim]

ABILITY LEVEL
Beginner

FINISHED SIZE
Individual to each blanket

RIBBONS
2.5cm/1in-width ribbon e.g. cream grosgrain used here – 2 x the finished length of the area of blanket to be trimmed

TOOLS
Medium "Sharp" needle

FABRIC
Natural wool blanket

OTHER MATERIALS
Matching thread

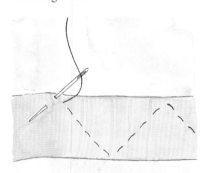

APPLYING THE RIBBON
1 Stitch a running stitch in a chevron pattern (see illustration above) along the desired length of ribbon.

2 Draw up the running stitch until the ribbon is gathered into a ruffle that is approximately half as long as the original flat ribbon.

3 Pin, baste and stitch the ruffle in place, approximately 12.5cm/5in from the end of the blanket, using running or back stitch, turning under each raw end of the trim neatly.

Contemporary blankets-3

[Rayon tape]

ABILITY LEVEL
Beginner

FINISHED SIZE
Individual to each blanket

RIBBONS
Woven tape that measures 2.5cm/1in wide – e.g. cream rayon used here, 2 x the finished length of the area of blanket to be trimmed

TOOLS
Medium "Sharp" needle

FABRIC
Natural wool blanket

OTHER MATERIALS
Matching thread

APPLYING THE RIBBON
1 Cut off the worn edges of the blanket.

2 Now fold the tape in half lengthways.

3 Pin, baste and slipstitch in place to cover the raw edge of the blanket, tucking in the raw ends of the tape neatly.

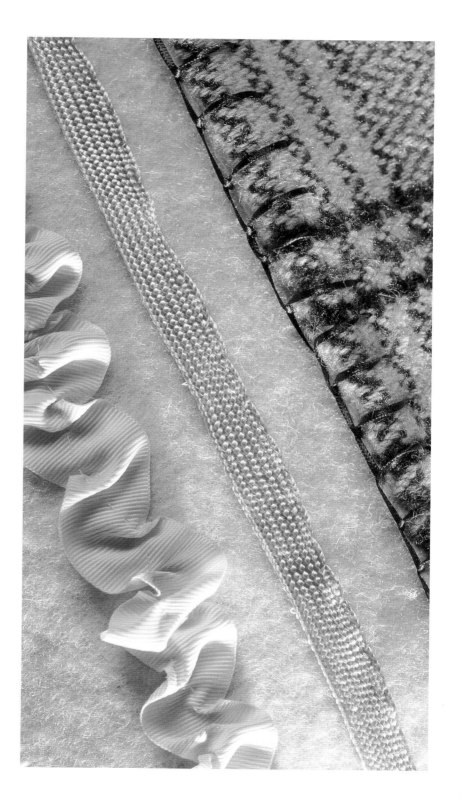

RIGHT The ruched frill, blanket stitch and rayon tape seen here on these blankets are all contemporary versions of traditional techniques of blanket edging.

Pansy nightdress case

This item recalls the 19th-century pastimes of fabric flowermaking and painting on velvet ribbons. Since ribbon flowermaking is enjoying a revival, I have included instructions for making the corsage of velvet ribbon pansies.

The charm of these flowers lies in their rather unsubtle colouring, and a certain naïveté to the finish. Note the raw edges on the circle of white velvet which provides a base for the pansies, and the carelessly wrapped stems of the flowers themselves.

Aim for a similarly unstudied result to achieve a nostalgic period feel, rather than attempting to produce realistic flowers. Alternatively, artificial flowers may be purchased from haberdashery, millinery, bridal and floristry departments.

Silk versions of dried flowers are now so convincing that a very sophisticated version of this project could be made. Substitute dried effect silk rosebuds for the pansies and use faded, floppy rayon ribbons in subtle shades for an elegant effect.

The posy sits on top of rows of gathered circles of satin ribbon, applied to a padded case. The decorated layer is produced first. Then the lining, backing and wadding layers are sandwiched together in such a way that after a single line of stitching the case is miraculously completed, save a few handstitches to close the gap where it is turned right side out.

If you are not making the flowers, this delightfully frou-frou project could be easily completed in an evening. As the flowers are not washable, the posy must be detached prior to laundering.

RIGHT Shamelessly feminine, the satin ribbon ruffles on this nightdress case, originally lurid violet and acid green, have been sunbleached to appealingly subtle shades. The sun has also degraded the ribbon texture considerably.

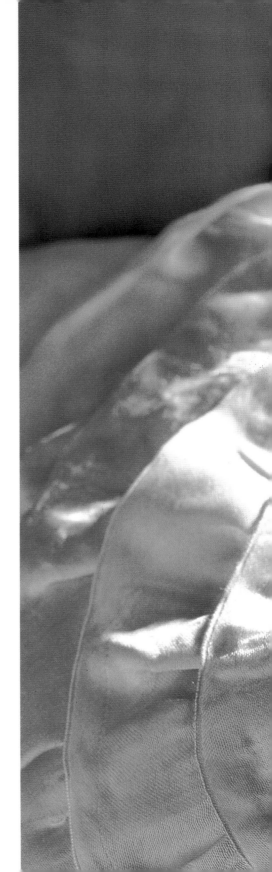

ABILITY LEVEL
Intermediate

FINISHED SIZE
36cm/14in diameter

RIBBONS
3.5m/4yd of 38mm/1⅛in pale lavender woven-edge satin

2.6m/3yd of 38mm/1⅛in white or very pale green woven-edge satin

1.1m/1¼yd of 38mm/1⅛in white velvet for pansies

1.9m/2¼yd of 38mm/1⅛in green cotton craft ribbon for leaves, calyxes and stems

TOOLS
Wire cutters

FABRIC
1 piece of pale lavender cotton, sufficient to make four circles each 39cm/15½in in diameter

1 piece of white velvet for centre, to make a circle approximately 5cm/2in diameter

OTHER MATERIALS
Lightweight wadding/batting, sufficient to make two circles each 39cm/15½in

Pale lavender silk thread

Fraycheck or other method of sizing fabric

Fabric/craft glue

FOR PANSIES:
Pencil or fade-out fabric marker, medium-gauge floristry wires, green florist's tape, four red/yellow

artificial stamens (from cake decorating shops or floristry suppliers), fabric pens or felt tipped pens in deep purple, yellow and black

[NB. Purchased, ready-made flowers may be substituted for the pansies]

STITCHES AND TECHNIQUES
• Slip stitch
• Making ribbon flowers
• Gathering
• Dyeing and painting
• Sizeing

MAKING UP
1 Cut four circles of lavender fabric and two circles of wadding/batting, each measuring 39cm/15½in in diameter.

Cut three lengths of lavender ribbon: 1 x 57cm/22½in, 1 x 114cm/45in, 1 x 171cm/67½in.

Cut three lengths of pale green ribbon: 1 x 29cm/11⅛in, 1 x 86cm/34in, 1 x 143cm/56½in.

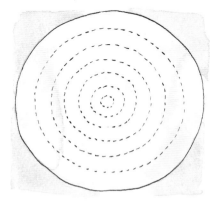

2 Using a pencil or fade-out pen, draw circles onto the right side of one of the pieces of lavender fabric following the illustration (above).

Construct the cushion front as follows: first, join the raw ends of each of the six lengths of ribbon (so that you have six ribbon circles) by stitching them together, with right sides facing, using a 1cm/⅜in seam allowance. Press seams open.

3 Run a gathering stitch along one edge of each of the ribbon circles. Then pull up the gathers evenly until each ribbon is the approximate size of the drawn circle on the initial piece of lavender fabric, marking its position on the front of the case.

4 Starting with the outermost lavender ribbon, pin and baste in place, making fine adjustments to the gathers as necessary. Stitch in place. Repeat this step with each ribbon in turn, alternating rings of green, then lavender, ribbon. Make sure that each new ribbon covers the previous stitch line. When each ribbon is secured, remove its gathering stitch.

5 Cut a circle of white velvet to cover the remaining lavender fabric centre. Treat the raw edges of the velvet with Fraycheck. Secure in place with a few central stitches.

6 Place the completed cushion front on a surface, right side up, on top of one of the circles of wadding/batting. Place the other pieces of fabric on top of the cushion front in the following order: lavender circle (right side down); wadding/batting circle; lavender circle (right side up); lavender circle (right side down).

7 Pin, baste and stitch through all the layers using a 1.5cm/⅝in seam allowance. Leave 25cm/10in unsewn for turning. Press seams open. Trim the wadding/batting close to the stitch line. Grade and clip the fabric seam allowances. Turn right side out.

8 Turn in the raw edges, and slipstitch each side of the lining to its neighbouring lavender circle to conceal the wadding/batting and produce a neatened opening for the nightdress case.

9 Follow the directions to make the posy of flowers in steps 1–8, or use purchased fabric flowers. Stitch the posy firmly to the circle of white velvet in the centre

of the cushion front. (See step 1, explaining how to make the posy.)

Making the flower posy

1 Cover the reverse of the white velvet ribbon and green cotton tape with Fraycheck or fabric glue. Leave to dry.

2 Following the templates provided below (reduce to 90%), and the photograph on page 59, draw petal shapes on the reverse of the white velvet ribbon, and leaf and calyx shapes on the green cotton tape. Cut out the calyxes. Glue a wire to the reverse of each leaf and each petal, as shown. Leave to dry. Cut out each petal and leaf. For each pansy: cut 3 x petal A, 2 x petal B and 1 x calyx. For the rolled bud: cut 1 x petal A, 1 x calyx. Cut three leaves in total.

3 Score veins onto the leaves using scissors. Colour the petals using fabric pens or felt-tipped pens.

4 To construct a flower you should tape a stamen to the end of a wire. Tape three (A) petals in place around the stem wire, followed by two (B) petals, allowing the stamen to protrude slightly in the middle of the pansy face.

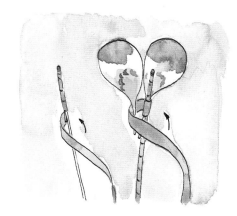

5 Trim the petal wires to different lengths so that they do not form an ungainly clump along the stem.

6 Apply tacky glue thinly to a strip of green cotton tape, and wind around each stem to cover all the wire ends, finishing under the base of each flower. Glue a calyx in place to cover the final join at the base of each flower.

7 To make a bud, roll an (A) petal into a cone and tape it onto a stem. Apply green cotton tape and a glued calyx as in step 5.

8 Tape the leaves onto the stems, using the photograph as a guide to placement.

9 Arrange the pansies in a posy and pull gently into shape.

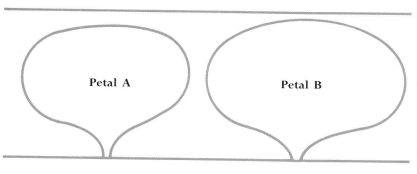

Petal A

Petal B

4cm/1½in

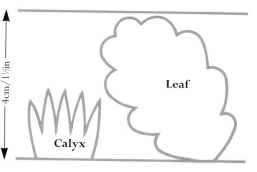

Leaf

Calyx

Cushions & Chair Pads

Companion cushion

Victorian embroiderers used ribbons in many different ways. As well as intricate surface embroidery, ribbons were woven through non-fraying materials. The regular nature of many lace patterns makes them ideally suited to ribbon weaving. This cushion utilises treasured scraps of lace, cotton and cotton lawn which have been laundered until they are exquisitely soft.

Although the finished cushion looks very fragile, it incorporates modern synthetic ribbons which will withstand quite heavy use. For a beginner, these ribbons are much simpler to weave than finer, more flexible silk. The very lack of flexibility in synthetic ribbons makes them less liable to twist and turn when they are woven – an especially important consideration when producing a rigidly geometric design such as this. To preserve the straight, crisp, trellis pattern, the ribbons need to lie perfectly flat when woven.

The sage green satin ribbon was chosen to pick out the traditional clover motif in the lace design. Experimenting with different ways of interlacing the ribbons produces delightfully varied results, depending upon the density of the lace, and how many holes the ribbon is carried over or passes beneath.

The cushion pad should be inserted into the cover before starting to weave, which will provide a perfect working base – softly padded, and held under just the right amount of tension to keep the work even. When purchasing materials for this project, make sure that the size of the holes in the lace matches the ribbon width exactly, so that the ribbon has space to spread comfortably, but is held sufficiently taut to maintain the woven pattern in daily use.

LEFT A crisp trellis of contemporary ombré ribbons weaves a fresh, summery pattern through a lace-fronted cushion.

ABILITY LEVEL
Beginner

FINISHED SIZE
48 x 48cm/19 x 19in

RIBBONS
3mm x 5m/⅛in x 5½yd lilac ombré for weaving across the lace panels

3mm x 4m/⅛in x 4yd lilac ombré for threading through frill, plus 50cm/19½in to tie off in a bow

3mm x 5m/⅛in x 5½yd sage-green woven-edge satin for weaving across lace panels

4cm x 38cm/1½in x 15in white woven-edge satin for central applied panel

3mm x 2m/⅛in x 2yd white woven-edge satin for bows to fasten cushion cover

TOOLS
Crewel needle with an eye of sufficient size to comfortably hold ribbon

FABRIC
8cm x 4m/3in x 4yd of lace-edged white cotton lawn for the frill

2 pieces of white cotton, each measuring 38 x 38cm/15 x 15in

38 x 38cm/15 x 15in of white lace with a regular design suitable for threading

1.5cm x 76cm/⅝in x 30in of white lace to edge central ribbon panel

OTHER MATERIALS
White thread

35cm/13¾in cushion pad

STITCHES AND TECHNIQUES
- Slip stitch
- French seam
- Sewing with ribbon
- Basic gathering stitch
- Threading ribbon
- Simple bow
- Ribbon weaving

MAKING UP
1 Press the cotton fabric and lace, so that they are square and even.

2 Assemble the cushion front in the following order:

Position the 38 x 38cm/15 x 15in lace on the 38 x 38cm/15 x 15in white cotton. Then lay 4cm/1½in white ribbon centrally across the lace. Pin and baste the pieces in position.

3 Position, pin and baste the 1.5cm/⅝in lace edging along either side of the ribbon panel to conceal the woven edges. Machine- or hand-stitch through all four layers, taking care to catch the edges of the ribbon.

French seam
4 A French seam is used in this project because it encloses all of the raw edges, with no additional stitches showing on the right side. Since both sides of the frill are visible on the finished project, this is an ideal choice.

Join the short ends of the lace-edged fabric for the frill using a French seam as follows:

With the wrong sides of the fabric facing each other, stitch a flat seam approximately 5mm/³⁄₁₆in from the edge of the fabric. Carefully trim the seam allowance to 3mm/⅛in. Turn the fabric back on itself so that the right sides of the fabric face each other. Now fold along the seam line, and press in place. Baste the two layers of fabric together, close to the folded edge. Stitch a second seam 1cm/⅜in from the folded edge, making sure that you enclose the raw edges. Then remove the basting stitches and unfold the fabric right side up. The neatened seam is now visible, with no other stitch line in evidence. Press the neatened seam allowance flat to one side of the seam.

5 Run a gathering stitch along the plain, long side of the lace-edged fabric for the frill.

To gather by hand
Using tiny back-stitches, fasten the thread in the fabric at one end of the stitch line. Sew a line of neat running stitches along the gathering line of the fabric, (approximately 1cm/½in from the edge of the fabric). When the last stitch meets the first, gently pull the thread, spacing the gathers evenly along the length of fabric until you achieve the required fullness. To gauge the exact finished length required, place a piece of string along the basting line on the cushion front, cut roughly to length, and knot the ends so that the string forms a continuous circle. Use this string circle as a size guide when pulling up the finished frill.

To gather by machine

Adjust the machine to its longest stitch and machine two rows of stitches along the gathering line of the fabric (approximately 1cm/½in from the fabric edge). Using the string technique described on the previous page, pull up the top stitches only until the frill is gathered roughly to the correct length.

6 Place the frill on the cushion front with right sides facing and the raw edges aligned. Adjust the frill to make the gathers even, allowing extra fullness at the corners so that the frill will fit comfortably when the cushion cover is turned right side out. Pin, then baste in place.

7 Pin and baste the remaining piece of fabric on top, with right side facing the cushion front. Stitch all around the cushion leaving a 25cm/10in opening in the middle of one side. Take care to avoid catching the frill in the line of stitching.

8 Stitch the frill to the cushion front along the 25cm/10in opening. Turn back 1.5cm/⅝in and hem the raw edges of the 25cm/10in opening using slip stitch.

9 Turn the cushion cover right side out. Insert the cushion pad.

10 Thread the needle with lilac ombré ribbon and bring through the fabric to the surface of the lace on the cushion front, locking off (see page 17 in the *Before You Begin* section) a soft knot on the reverse of the cotton fabric to begin.

11 Stitching through the lace only, weave the ribbon through the design. Work methodically, weaving all the lines travelling in one direction first, alternating the under and over movement of the weave with each new ribbon line. Take care to keep the tension even and make sure that the ribbon lies flat. Finish by locking off with a soft knot on the reverse.

12 Weave the sage-green ribbon through the lace as in step 11.

13 Hand-stitch four 3mm x 25cm/¼ x 10in white ribbons 5cm/2in apart, on each side of the opening to make

ties. Tie each pair in a simple bow to close the cushion.

14 Starting at one corner, use the crewel needle to thread the lilac ombré ribbon around the lace-edged frill, and tie off in a bow.

Ribbon cushion

In the late 19th century, ribbon embroidery – also known as rococo work – was a particularly popular form of decoration for mats and runners. I found a very good example of it – an embroidered runner – in an antiques shop in London, England, and knew that it would make a perfect gift for a friend who adores antique textiles.

Without disturbing any of the original work, I made the runner into this satisfyingly oversized moiré cushion, trimmed with a subtle self-coloured fringe. Since runners already occupy every available surface in any textile collector's home, new ways to display acquisitions are always welcomed.

The combination of buttercup- and lemon-yellow ribbons with sage- and grass-greens, embroidered on a cream background, has produced a design that is as fresh as a field of daisies. Just as in a real field, the colours and textures of this design are so closely matched as to be almost indistinguishable from one another, until one studies the individual components closely. Choose ribbons and threads that almost blend into each other, for a similarly impressionistic result.

French knots and satin stitches in single glossy strands of thread add textural interest without detracting from the delicacy of the ribbon work. The original gold thread, couched in place with tiny stitches to form the stems, has tarnished to dull black. For a subtle, aged look, replace the gold threads specified with pewter-toned ones.

RIGHT Discovered in an English antique shop in its original form of a runner, this ribbon-embroidered rectangle of moiré taffeta makes a pleasingly oversized cushion.

ABILITY LEVEL
Intermediate

FINISHED SIZE
70cm x 50cm/27½ x 19¾in
including fringe

RIBBONS
Pale green/gray to white silk
3.5mm/⅛in wide

Dark forest-green ombré
silk 4mm/⅛in wide

Pale yellow-green ombré silk
4mm/⅛in wide

Golden-yellow ombré silk
3.5mm/⅛in wide

Pale yellow ombré silk
4mm/⅛in wide

TOOLS
Chenille needle
(for ribbon embroidery)

Fine crewel needle
(for thread embroidery)

FABRIC
Two pieces of cream moiré
taffeta, each measuring 73cm x
53cm/28½ x 20¾in

OTHER MATERIALS
Gold metallic thread and
a slightly finer gold metallic
thread

6-strand gold-brown embroidery
cotton DMC 437/Anchor 362
(use single strand)

6-strand embroidery cotton DMC
3078/Anchor 292 (use single strand)
or pale yellow silk embroidery
thread

6-strand embroidery cotton
(use single strand) DMC 972/
Anchor 362 or fine golden-yellow
silk embroidery thread

6-strand gold-green embroidery
cotton (use single strand) DMC
3045/Anchor 888

2.43m/95½in of 2.5cm/1cm-wide
cream fringe

Cushion pad 50 x 70cm/
27½ x 19¾in

Polyester cotton thread to match
moiré and fringe

STITCHES AND TECHNIQUES
• Satin stitch
• Straight stitch
• French knots
• Slip stitch

MAKING UP
1 Press the fabric to make sure that
it is square and even. Press on
the reverse of the fabric, using
a pressing cloth.

2 Transfer the design.

Couching
3 Throughout the history of
embroidery, threads have been
couched for two main reasons:
either because they are too
sturdy to pass easily through
the fabric without distorting it, or –
as on many religious pieces
like this – for reasons of
economy when using expensive
gold or silver threads. Laying
the gold thread flat on one surface
of the fabric only obviously uses
far less thread. To embroider
the metallic, couched stems:
cut a length of metallic thread

to approximately the finished
length required on the surface
of the fabric. Thread it through
an appropriately sized crewel
needle, and bring the metallic
thread through the fabric,
from the back to the front –
at the beginning of each of the
stitch lines.

4 Thread a finer needle with
a single strand of six-strand
embroidery cotton, or fine silk
thread, and secure the metallic
thread in place along the stitch
line, using tiny stitches to hold
it firmly.

5 Embroider the small circular
motifs and sprigs in satin stitch
(see page 18 in the *Before You Begin*
section), using a single strand of
embroidery cotton, or silk thread.

6 Stitch the ribbon-embroidered
flowers in straight stitch (see page
19), working the larger petals first.
Stitch a subsequent row of smaller
petals in straight stitch on top of this
first layer.

7 Stitch the ribbon-embroidered
leaves in straight stitch. Take care to
keep the ribbon as flat and well-
spread on the surface of the fabric
as possible.

8 Stitch the French knot flower
centres in embroidery thread.

9 Place the two pieces of moiré
fabric together, with right sides
facing. Pin, baste and machine-
stitch together using a 1.5cm/½in
seam allowance. Leave a gap large
enough for turning. Turn the cushion
cover right side out, and insert
the pad.

10 Press the seams open.

11 Turn the cushion cover right side out and slipstitch closed. Alternatively, you could neatly turn a double hem at each of the remaining raw edges and hand-stitch to secure.

12 Stitch touch-and-close fastening or snap fasteners in place on each side, so that the cushion cover is easily removable for laundering.

13 Slipstitch the fringe around the cushion edge, turning under the raw ends of the fringe neatly.

ADAPTING THE DESIGN

A few lazy daisies sprinkled on a pillowcase would make a delightfully fresh motif. Choose white ribbons on white linen for a sophisticated effect. For pillow cases that need frequent laundering, it is sensible to use cotton or rayon ribbons, rather than silk, which may not be very durable.

COLOUR KEY
Thread/ribbon type/stitch

Ombré silk ribbon; straight

Silk thread; DMC972/Anch 362

DMC 972/Anch 298; 3078/292

Fine metallic thread; couched

3.5mm/⅛in ombré silk ribbon

DMC 437/Anchor 362; Fr. kn.

Thick gold metallic thread

Ombré silk ribbon

Ombré ribbon; straight stitch

Ombré silk ribbon

Cushion trimmings

These pretty cushions were found in a country antiques market in Wiltshire, England. I was attracted to their subtle colouring and the trailing ribbon motif. Although made of new fabric, they looked perfectly at home on a Regency sofa covered in its original silk damask. It is not always practical to use antique fabrics for soft furnishings; their fragility can mean that they simply will not withstand the rigours of daily use. We have shown here how to personalize new cushions using inventive ribbon trims, this is an easy way to enhance contemporary textiles so that they can be combined happily .

Making your own trimmings and braids is immensely satisfying. I have admired similar, intricately pleated and plaited edgings in trimmings specialists' shops, but find the cost per metre or yard prohibits their use in all but the smallest scale of sewing projects. It is thrilling to produce something so spectacular from just a few metres of inexpensive satin ribbon and with relatively little effort. Following the basic techniques, using ribbons of varied widths, colours and textures, you will be able to produce trims that can be used to edge all manner of soft furnishings.

Although complex in appearance, these edgings are very quick and simple to make and therefore ideal as a project for a beginner.

LEFT AND ABOVE Braided and pleated ribbons make wonderfully flexible trimmings which turn the corners of these cushion covers with ease. Deceptively elaborate in appearance, these trimmings are in fact quick and easy to make.

Braided cushion trim

ABILITY LEVEL
Beginner

FINISHED SIZE
2cm/¾in-wide braid x 164cm/64½in

RIBBONS
7mm/⅛in x 9 times the perimeter
of cushion, plus an additional
27cm/10½in for joining, of silver
gray, double-face, woven-edge satin.

[This cushion requires 7mm x
15m/⅛in x 50yd]

TOOLS
Medium "Sharp" needle

FABRIC
Brocade-covered cushion

OTHER MATERIALS
Thread to match ribbon

STITCHES AND TECHNIQUES
• Slip stitch
• Braiding

MAKING UP
1 Fold the length of ribbon in
half to find the centre. Pinch
the ribbon lightly at this point –
this will give you your centre
mark.

2 Place the ribbon on the surface
with the loose tails facing you,
and the lightly folded centre
mark centrally in front of you,
facing away.

3 Hold the right tail of the
ribbon in your right hand and
pass it over the left-hand tail to
make a loop. Do not twist the
ribbon. In braiding, the strands

to be woven together remain
upward-facing; it is only in plaiting
that the strands are allowed to turn,
forming a rounded rather than
flat finish.

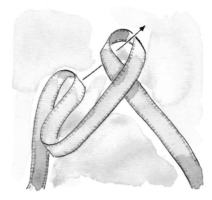

4 Form a loop in the tail that is
now on the left (see illustration).

5 Insert the folded edge of the
loop that you have just made
through the first loop, passing
from the back of the loop to
the front.

6 Now you should gently pull
the tail on the right until it is
sufficiently tight to hold the loop
firmly, but do not pull so tightly
that the ribbon becomes puckered.
You now have a new loop at the
top of the work.

7 Form a loop in the tail that is
now on the right, and insert this
loop through the loop at the top
of the work (see step 6). Gently
pull the tail that is now on the
left to hold the new loop in place.

8 Continue making loops, following
steps 5 and 6, alternating from left
to right in this way.

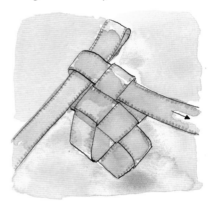

Carry on until you reach the ends
of the ribbon tails. Take particular
care to maintain an even tension as
you braid, and make sure that the
ribbon remains untwisted and
unpuckered as it is worked.

Finishing
9 To finish, tuck the loose ends
of each ribbon tail into the braid.
Hand-stitch neatly to secure.

10 The finished braid is
very flexible, and perfect
for trimming curves. Place
the beginning end of the braid
centrally along one side of the
cushion cover, rather than fixing
it at a corner.

11 Slipstitch the trim around the
perimeter of the cushion cover,
concealing stitches within the bottom
layer of the braid.

Ruffled cushion trim

ABILITY LEVEL
Intermediate

FINISHED SIZE
2cm/¾in-wide ruffle x length of cushion perimeter [length of perimeter is 164cm/64½in on this cushion], plus 3cm/1in allowance for joining

RIBBONS
20mm/¾in x 4 times perimeter of cushion, plus 12cm/4¾in for joining, in sage-green

10mm/¼in x 4 times perimeter of cushion, plus 12cm/4¾in, in silver-gray

3mm/⅛in x 1 times perimeter of cushion, plus 3cm/1in, in sage-green – all in double-face, woven-edge satin.

[This cushion requires 20mm x 7m/¾in x 7 ½yd in sage-green, 10mm x 7m/¼in x 7½yd in silver-gray, and 3mm x 1.70m/⅛in x 2yd in sage-green]

TOOLS
Medium "Sharp" needle

FABRIC
Brocade-covered cushion

OTHER MATERIALS
Thread to match sage-green ribbon

MAKING UP
1 Machine- or hand-stitch the 10mm/¼in ribbon in place centrally along the face of the 20mm/¾in ribbon, along its length.

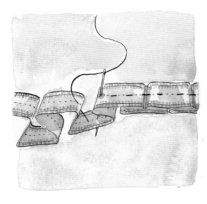

2 Practise box-pleating the layered ribbon, until you achieve a size of pleat which looks appropriate to the width of the ribbon. When you are comfortable with the technique, box-pleat the layered ribbon by hand, securing each pleat using back stitch.

3 Place the 3mm/⅛in ribbon centrally on the face of the layered and pleated ribbons, along the length.

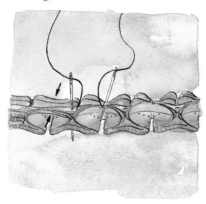

4 Stitch as follows:
Bring the needle through all three layers of ribbon, from back to front, at the centre of a pleat. Then pinch together the edges of the 20mm/¾in ribbon and secure with two tiny overcasting stitches. Now return the needle through these stitches, back through the three layers of ribbon.

Make sure that you preserve the height of the pinched pleat.

5 Bring the needle up through the three layers of ribbon, between the pleats, and secure with a tiny stitch. Repeat steps 3 & 4 along the length of the ribbon layers in this way.

6 Starting at the centre of one edge of the cushion, stitch the trim around the edge of the cushion, hand-stitching only through the 20mm/¾in ribbon, making sure that the stitch is not visible on the surface of the trim.

7 Where the raw ends of the trim meet, turn under and stitch neatly to each other, and onto the cushion.

NB. This trim produces a delightfully pronounced ruffle that is best left unpressed.

FINISHING
For a spectacular baroque finish, tiny clear glass rocaille beads may be incorporated into this trim at step 4. The sparkling beads catch the light at the apex or each pinched pleat, producing a charming fairytale finish.

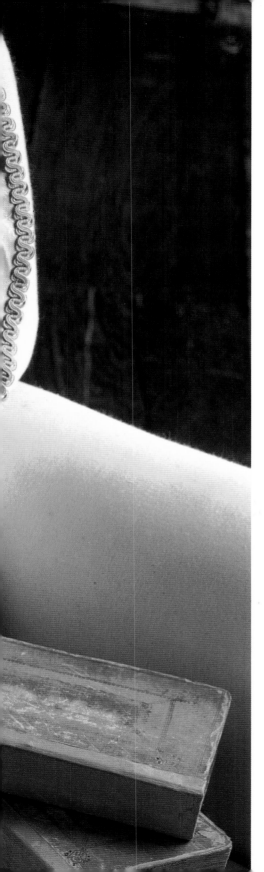

Chair back

Ecclesiastical embroidery has long been a rich repository of highly elaborate needlework designs. This 19th-century ribbon-embroidered piece was originally part of a religious garment – the main section of which has long since perished. The embroidery, far too beautiful to discard, has been mounted onto a firm backing fabric for use as a beautifully ornate chair back.

Since the Middle Ages, many people have believed that gifts to the church prepare a foundation for rewards in heaven. Indeed, the quality of the stitching on many ecclesiastical pieces is quite often faultless. Perhaps this accounts for the incredibly meticulous stitching on this chair back.

The stitches which couch the metallic threads in place are so tiny that they are invisible to the naked eye. In order to identify the other stitches in this design, a powerful magnifying glass was needed. Even then, the stitches were so small and neat as to be barely discernible. Under the closest scrutiny, there is simply not a single stitch out of place. This is an example of quite staggering needle skills and patience.

Here, the floral motif and central section has been reproduced (on the following pages). It is a delightfully pretty design that could actually be adapted for use in many soft furnishings – around a curtain tie-back or as a table runner, for example. The ribbon embroidery itself is reasonably quick to work, and is given an opulent finish by the outline of metallic thread. For a more restrained appearance, and to achieve a result more quickly, the couched outline could be omitted.

LEFT Exemplary embroidery skills are displayed in this elaborate piece. To match the breathtaking quality of the original is a challenge for an experienced needleworker.

ABILITY LEVEL
Advanced

FINISHED SIZE
Approximately 56 x 61cm/22 x 24in

RIBBONS
Green ombré 3mm/⅛in silk ribbon for leaves

Pink ombré 3mm/⅛in silk ribbon for flowers

A small length of plain yellow 3mm/⅛in silk ribbon for flower centres

TOOLS
Chenille needle for ribbon embroidery

Fine crewel needle for sequins and other embroidery

FABRIC
A piece of ivory silk damask measuring approximately 59 x 64cm/23 x 25in

A piece of heavy ivory backing fabric approximately 59 x 64cm/23 x 25in

OTHER MATERIALS
Small and large gold sequins

Flat "old gold" braid to trim edge 1.5cm/⅝in width (measuring approximately 2.5m/2¾yd)

Metallic threads:
Kreinik (Coats) gold Japan ribbon ⅟₁₆in wide (there is no DMC alternative available)

Kreinik (Coats) antique gold special blend thread 221 (DMC gold 276)

Kreinik (Coats) gold Japan thread

No.5 (DMC Art 280 gold)

Kreinik (Coats) Diadem 300 gold (there is no DMC equivalent available)

Stranded embroidery cotton (use 2 strands only):
Pale pink, DMC 3713/ Anchor 1020

Yellow-green, DMC 3013/ Anchor 842

Dark green, DMC 367/ Anchor 217

Silk thread:
dark green, burgundy, natural, golden

STITCHES AND TECHNIQUES
• Slip stitch
• Chain stitch
• Stem stitch
• Sewing with ribbon

MAKING UP
1 Press the fabric and transfer the design. On the following pages templates are provided for the main floral pattern (which is repeated), and the central border. Use the plan provided on page 80 for the correct placement of the design. Reduce templates to 75%.

2 Embroider the metallic couched design, and those parts of the design worked in embroidery threads and silk thread; all except the threads which outline the ribbon leaves and flowers. [NB. The green inner outline on page 83 is DMC 3013/Anchor 832 – stem stitch. The same green thread has been used here on the "mitre" motifs – in padded satin stitch.]

3 Stitch the ribbon embroidery.

4 Stitch couched metallic outlines around the ribbon embroidery.

5 Stitch on the sequins using natural silk thread. Thread a short length of Diadem gold thread onto the thread which appears on the surface of the sequin, to prevent it being pulled straight back through.

6 Mark out the desired shape of the finished chair back, placing the embroidery centrally and leaving a 1.5cm/⅝in seam allowance. Mark out an identical piece of backing fabric.

7 Turn under and gently press the seam allowance on each piece of fabric. Slipstitch together, wrong sides facing.

8 Stitch flat braid around the perimeter of the chair back, turning under raw ends neatly.

NOTE: The finished chair back is an heirloom piece that is best professionally dry cleaned or handwashed in fine soap. Check the manufacturer's details when purchasing metallic threads, as these may be adversely affected by some dry cleaning solvents and detergents.

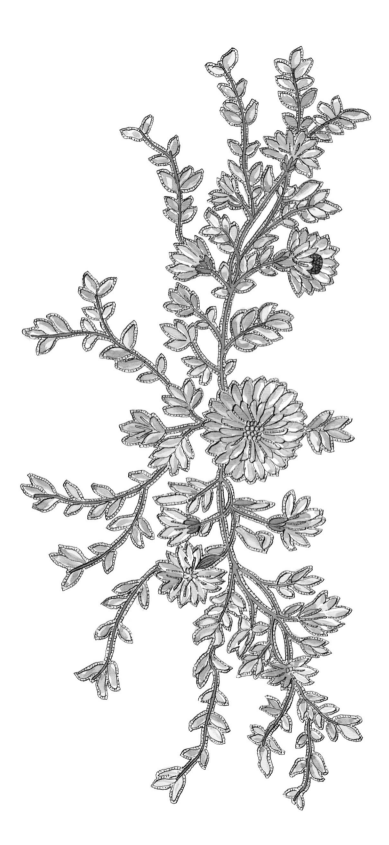

Colour key

Thread/ribbon type/stitch

- Gold sequins (2 sizes)
- Kreinik (Coats) antique gold
- Kreinik (Coats) Japan ribbon
- Kreinik (Coats) Diadem 300
- Kreinik (Coats) Japan no.5 gold
- Ombré ribbon
- Silk ribbon for flower centre
- 3mm/⅛in ombré silk ribbon
- Silk ribbon (p.82)/thread (p.83)
- Silk thread; chain stitch
- Anchor 1020/DMC 3713; stem
- Ombré ribbon for flowers

Braided seat pad

This delightful seat pad was discovered at an English country antiques fair. Essentially a folk art piece, it has a definite colonial feel to it. Early colonists had little to brighten their homes, and saved every scrap of used and worn material for recycling. After clothes had outlived their original purpose they were passed down, or remade into clothes for the next in line in the family. The worn scraps were scrupulously hoarded, and eventually found their way into braided rugs and seat pads.

Some braided mats and rugs were meticulously planned, shading from a light middle to a dark border for example, but this seat pad has classically thrifty origins, utilising whatever came to hand during its making. The mat is largely composed, unusually, of ribbon. It is an ideal project for utilizing all those scraps of ribbon and braid that you cannot quite bear to discard. Velvet, petersham, satin, linen, cotton and rayon, all make an appearance. To maintain an overall tonal balance, choose one light, one medium and one dark strand as you braid.

The braids have been somewhat clumsily stitched together – an authentic method of constructing a braided mat, but not one that I would recommend. Lacing the braids together is stronger and has the added bonus of making the pad reversible as no threads show on either surface. Waxed thread has been used on this mat, but is both too strong and too bold for such fine fabrics. If the pad were to be tugged carelessly, it would be desirable that just the thread snap, rather than remaining intact and tearing through the braid. Silk thread is recommended as a viable alternative. For a more substantial result, this project could be worked in woollen tapes.

LEFT Scraps of ribbons of all textures and colours produce a charmingly random pattern in this braided seat pad.

ABILITY LEVEL
Intermediate

FINISHED SIZE
38 x 40.5cm/15 x 16in

RIBBONS
A total of approximately 50m/54yd of assorted ribbons each 5cm/2in wide, including rayon, petersham, velvet, cotton, satin, viscose

NB. This project could also be worked in woollen tapes for a more substantial result, suitable for a small rug. Most larger braided rugs were constructed from strips of old clothes. Heavy or medium-weight woollens make pleasingly substantial rugs. Before using recycled clothes, unpick the seams, remove linings, zips, pockets etc. and launder. Allow to dry naturally. Do not tumble dry woollens, as few second-hand woven woollens will resist matting when treated in this way. [Hold the fabric to a bright window to check visually for signs of wear or moth damage. Discard any damaged areas of the fabric as these would weaken the finished rug or chair pad.]

TOOLS
Safety pins

Blunt tapestry needle

Pins

Medium "Sharp" needle

Three braid aids* (available from Clotilde mail order)

Table top clamp* (available from Clotilde mail order)
(* optional)

OTHER MATERIALS
Neutral colour silk thread

STITCHES AND TECHNIQUES
• Slip stitch
• Braiding
• Overcasting

MAKING UP
1 Divide the ribbons into three groups according to tone: light, medium and dark. Use one strip of each tone when making the braid.

2 The most comfortable braiding length for each strip is approximately 3m/3¼yd. If you need to join ribbons and tapes to make suitable lengths, join the short ends using a bias seam as follows:

Making a bias seam
Place one strip on top of the other at a right angle to the first, right sides facing. Stitch diagonally across the strips to join them. Although the strips can be seamed together by hand, machine-stitching adds strength to the finished braid. Work with ribbons of slightly differing lengths so that all the joins do not occur next to each other, forming unsightly bumps in the finished braid.

Preparing the strips
3 Accurate folding is the key to successful braiding. All the strips must be neatly folded, concealing the edges, to produce an even finish. Although it is possible to fold as you braid, prefolding is recommended for the most consistent results until you are experienced.

A. Prefolding strips by hand
Fold the edges of each ribbon to the centre. Bring the new, folded edges together so that the strip has four layers. It is vital to fix the folds in place as they are made. Try not to press the folded ribbons with an iron, as this would make the finished pad too compressed. However, if you are making a mat from heavier woollen tape, or sturdy fabric strips, you could very lightly press the folds to secure them as you work. When working with ribbons, a gentler method is to pin, then baste the folds in place as they are formed.

B. Folding as you braid
The simplest method of folding as you braid is to use a braid-aid. This invaluable device is not widely available in the U.K., but is stocked in most American haberdashery departments. (Or mail order internationally from Clotilde USA.) A braid aid is similar to the device used for making bias binding, but accepts wider strips of fabric or ribbon. These useful tools have been developed to enable the automatic folding of strips as they are braided. You may like to experiment with a binding maker if a braid aid is not available. Choose a size compatible with your ribbon width, and test that the ribbons and tapes you wish to use will pass smoothly through the slots. You will need a braid aid or binding marker for each strip. Place each strip in each braid aid binding maker, and slide the tool down each strip as you braid. Roll each folded ribbon into a tight coil as you work, to maintain the folds. Dampen each coil by dipping each side lightly into a saucer of water 3mm/⅛in deep. Blot dry on a clean towel and leave in a warm place to dry thoroughly. Secure each coil with a safety pin.

4 Release approximately 1m/39in from each of the three coils, leaving the remainder pinned in place. Partially unfold the ends of two of the strips. Join with right sides facing, using a bias seam.

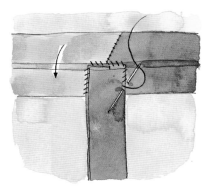

5 With the two joined ribbons half opened out, wrong sides facing, place the end of the third folded ribbon, with its open edge facing left, centrally on the bias seam of the joined ribbons so that the three ribbons form a "T" shape. Stitch neatly in place. Re-fold ribbons closed to conceal newly joined end.

6 To hold the ribbon ends firmly in place as you braid you can tack the joined strip to a board placed in front of you. Alternatively, use a small tabletop clamp. Begin

braiding by passing the right-hand strip over the centre strip twelve times in succession, making what are known as "modified turns".

Modified turns

These turns increase the loops on one side of the braid so that the strands continue to appear evenly braided, even when forming the tightly turned centre of the mat, after which a normal straight braid will turn sufficiently to negotiate the radius without twisting. Instead of straight braiding, lift the right strand over the centre strand, the new right strand over the new centre strand, the new centre strand over the new centre strand again, then the new right strand over the new centre strand a final, third time. Tightly place the centre strand down and continue braiding normally.

How braiding differs from plaiting

In braiding, the thumbnails are kept facing upward, so that the braid stays flat, rather than as in plaiting where the wrist is twisted, allowing the strips to form a round rope rather than a flat braid. Keep the open edge of the fold facing left at all times, to produce a neat result.

7 After the initial modified turns required at the centre of the pad, continue using straight stitch.

Straight braiding

Pass the right-hand strip over the centre strip, then the left-hand strip over the new centre strip; continue

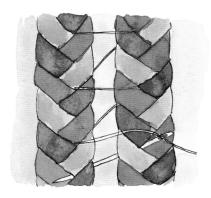

straight braiding, maintaining an even tension throughout.

8 When 1m/39in has been braided, lace the mat together (see illustration above), using silk thread in a blunt tapestry needle. Lace with the open folds facing the centre of the mat, threading between the strips, up through one loop, and down through the adjacent loop in a movement similar to overcasting. Continue braiding and lacing in this way.

Tapering the ends

9 Approximately 15cm/6in from where the pad will end, put aside the strips leaving a 50cm/19¾in length. Unfold each of the strips in turn. Make a cut along each one, beginning at the centre of the raw end, graduating to the full width at the point where you stopped braiding. When each strip has been cut in this way, from the central point, diagonally, twice to the full width where braiding ended – refold the strips and continue lacing.

10 Continue lacing the tapered braid. Weave the remaining strips into the outer braid of the mat, adding each one at a slightly different place to avoid creating a bump. Slipstitch firmly in position.

Accessories & Gifts

Ribbon roses basket

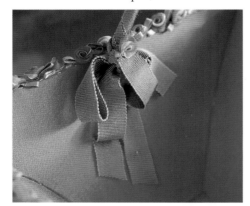

Roses fashioned from ribbon have trimmed garments and soft furnishings since Victorian times. Once you have mastered the basic technique, ribbon roses can be constructed in a myriad of sizes, colours and textures to add a romantic finishing touch to everything from soft furnishings to millinery. The ninety small organdy roses which ramble around the rim of this silk and lace basket, are made from randomly patterned ribbon, which gives them a wonderfully sculptural quality. There are skilled crafts people who specialize in creating small quantities of these inspiring, hand-dyed ribbons. Alternatively, it is very satisfying to paint and dye your own ribbons. Instructions are given in the *Before You Begin* section at the front of this book (see page 16). Commercially dyed patterned ribbon will give equally attractive variations in tone.

When purchasing ribbons for this project, it is worth taking into account that it is the variety of textures used, as well as the delicate colouring, that makes this basket so visually arresting. The handle is wrapped in rather masculine-looking matt grosgrain; a sophisticated foil to the frivolous organdy roses. In turn, the translucency of the ribbon used for the roses is offset by the use of glossy satin to form simple representations of leaves.

RIGHT AND ABOVE Tiny organdy ribbon roses blossom around the rim and trail up the grosgrain ribbon-wrapped handle of a decorative basket. Each rose sits on top of a fold of narrow satin ribbon.

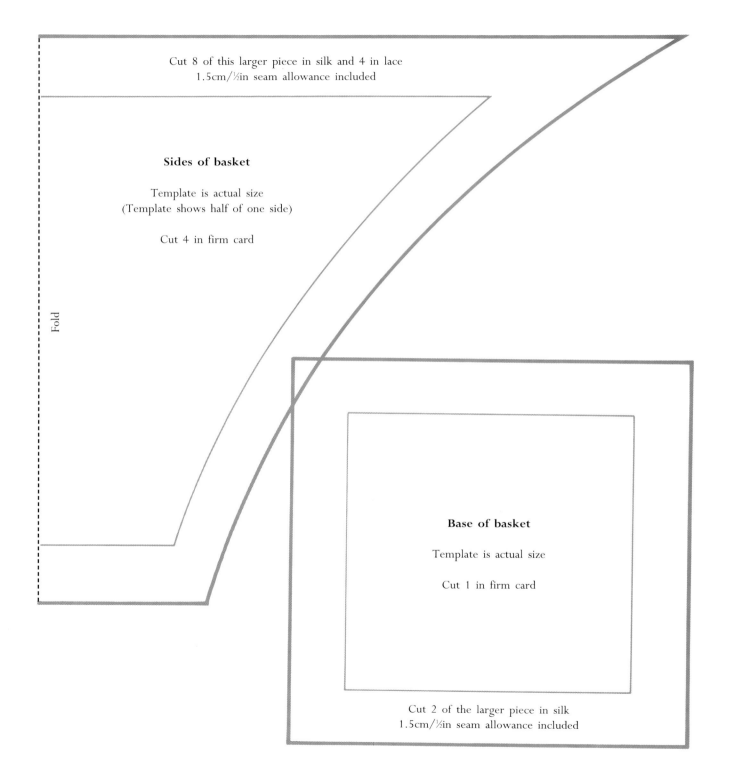

Cut 8 of this larger piece in silk and 4 in lace
1.5cm/½in seam allowance included

Sides of basket

Template is actual size
(Template shows half of one side)

Cut 4 in firm card

Fold

Base of basket

Template is actual size

Cut 1 in firm card

Cut 2 of the larger piece in silk
1.5cm/½in seam allowance included

ABILITY LEVEL Intermediate

FINISHED SIZE
25 x 25cm/10 x 10in

RIBBONS
1.5cm/⅝in x 1m/1⅛yd wide
dull-green grosgrain for wrapping
handle and tying bow

Organdy ribbon for roses 1cm/⅜in-
wide – 7cm/2¾in for each rose

Double-face woven-edge green satin
ribbon 3mm/⅛in wide – 6cm/2¾in
for each rose

TOOLS Medium "Sharp" needle

FABRIC
Sufficient mulberry-coloured silk to
cover an area 2.5m x 15cm/2¾yd
x 6in

One piece of lace 1m x 15cm/1⅛yd
x 6in

2.5m/2¾yd of lace 1.5cm/⅝in wide

OTHER MATERIALS
Thread to match lace/silk/ribbons

Purchased artificial leaves (from
floristry or cake-decorating suppliers
or millinery departments)

One piece of thick cardboard 1m
x 15cm/1⅛yd x 6in

Supple twig for handle or length
of plastic tubing (from DIY stores),
50cm/19¾in long

MAKING UP
1 Press the silk and lace.

2 Transfer the pattern pieces onto
the fabric and cardboard.

3 To make each side of the basket:
place two pieces of silk together,
right sides facing. Pin, baste, and
stitch together along the two vertical
sides, and the short base side. Clip
curves and press seams open.

4 Turn right side out; insert
cardboard. Slipstitch the silk closed
to enclose the cardboard. Repeat
for each of the four sides.

5 Then place the two squares of silk
for the base together, right sides
facing. Pin, baste and stitch together
on three sides. Press seams open.
Turn right side out and insert
cardboard. Slipstitch the silk closed
to encapsulate the card. Slipstitch the
sides/base pieces together.

6 To make the handle: from the
remaining scraps of silk cut bias
strips as long as possible, each
2.5cm/1in wide to make a bias
strip approximately 2m/2¼yd long in
total. If necessary, join shorter strips
together, right sides facing, to make
a strip of sufficient length.

7 Press long sides of strips toward
the middle, concealing raw edges.
Wrap the strips tightly around the
twig or plastic tube. Secure with
tiny stitches. Slipstitch the lace
panels together over exterior of the
basket. Slipstitch narrow lace around
each side of basket to conceal seams.

8 **Leaves:** Fold in each end of a
6cm/2¾in length of 3mm/⅛in-wide
green satin ribbon so that the ends
overlap slightly. Stitch to secure,
using the silk thread which matches
silk fabric. Leave needle threaded.

9 **Roses:** Fold a 1cm/⅜in-wide
7cm/2¾in length of organdy ribbon

in half lengthwise. Roll one end
into a tight cone. Stitch to
secure through open folded edge
of the cone. Pull thread tight so
that centre of rose sits on centre of
the pair of leaves. Continue rolling
the ribbon around the central cone,
twisting to form a realistic rose
shape. Stitch to secure as you roll
and twist.

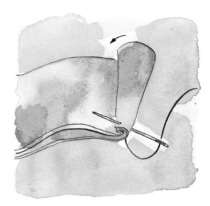

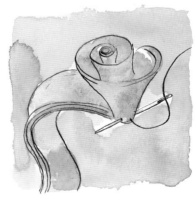

10 Wrap a 50cm/19¾in length
of green grosgrain ribbon around
the handle, and stitch to secure.
Using the remaining ribbon, tie a
bow around one side of the
handle and stitch the tails in place
to secure.

11 Stitch roses in place around rim
of basket and onto the handle. Stitch
artificial leaves in place on handle.

Appliqué basket

This basket has long been a source of exquisite torment for me. Filled with eggs from a local farm, it sits on the counter of an antique shop that I visit regularly. The eggs are for sale. The basket, despite my endless pleas to the contrary, is unfortunately not. I am delighted, however, that is immortalised in print here.

The silk is delectably crisp to the touch, and its sorbet of green, lemon and vanilla colouring are as fresh and cheering as the first flowers of Spring. The striking candy-bright shades of

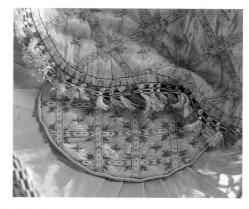

the trellis of appliquéd ribbons, and the very simple thread embroidery, remain vivid in the lining of the basket. On the ribbon twined around the handle, however, the ribbons seem to have have faded to sherbet tones on the padded silk lid .

Details for replicating both the faded and the vivid colourings are provided on page 96. You can mix the two – as shown – or select one scheme only. Overleaf you will also find a template for the basket, while the complete design has been reproduced on page 97.

It is important to remember, when appliquéing ribbons, to always stitch along both woven edges in the same direction; this will avoid unsightly and puckering.

LEFT Protected beneath its quilted lid from the blanching effects of the sun, these appliquéd ribbons retain their original vivid colours.
ABOVE Detail of the trellis of appliquéd ribbons.

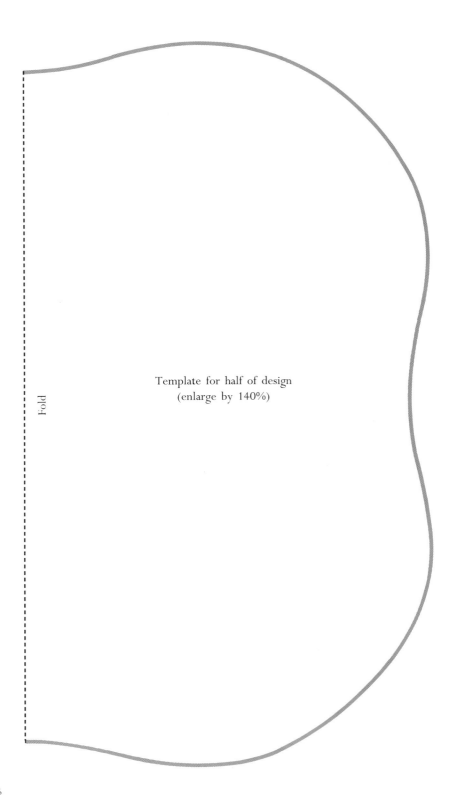

Fold

Template for half of design
(enlarge by 140%)

ABILITY LEVEL Intermediate

FINISHED SIZE
25 x 26cm/10 x 10¼in

RIBBONS
5mm/¼in embroidered ribbons:

1m/1¼yd to wind around handle

1m/1¼yd to cover interior
perimeter seam

1.20m/1½yd to criss-cross appliqué
bottom central disk

For lid: 3.30m/3¾yd of the same
ribbon to criss-cross appliqué

For lid perimeter: 1m/1¼yd of
5mm/¼in-wide ribbon with
2.5cm/1in depth candy-pink,
lime-green, white and primrose-
yellow fringe

TOOLS
Medium "Sharp" and embroidery
needles

FABRIC
1 piece yellow silk 26 x 27cm/
10¼ x 10¾in for face of lid

1 piece ivory silk 26 x 27cm/
10¼ x 10¾in for reverse of lid

1 piece pale green silk 90cm/
approx x 14cm/35½ x 5½in to
line basket

1 oval of pale green silk 11 x
11.5cm/4¼ x 4½in (finished size),
plus a small amount of bias cut
fabric for piping this central base pad

OTHER MATERIALS
Embroidery threads: Bright green
DMC Broder Spécial no 911,

candy-pink DMC Pearl cotton 891 [These original, vivid shades are visible in the padded circle in the basket lining, but the colours on the basket lid have faded considerably. To recreate these faded tones, substitute DMC Broder Spécial 471 for the bright green and DMC pearl cotton 224 for the candy-pink]

Silk thread to tone with appliquéd ribbon

1 piece of lightweight wadding/batting 24 x 25cm/9½ x 10 and 1 oval of wadding/batting 11 x 11.5cm/4¼ x 4½in diameter

MAKING UP

1 Press all fabrics so that they are square and even.

2 For the lining: cut a strip of green silk to fit the perimeter of the basket, plus a 1.5cm/½in seam allowance. Place short sides facing together. Pin, baste and stitch a seam. Press open. Turning under the raw edge, slipstitch in place at the top of the basket. Run a gathering stitch around the raw edge of the lining and pull into shape, forming neat folds to fit the curves of the basket interior. Stitch narrow ribbon around perimeter of basket lining, using running stitch, tucking under raw edges where they meet.

3 To make the padded base of the basket liner: cut out an oval to fit the base as follows: one in green silk, one in lightweight wadding. Appliqué ribbons in place following the photograph. Note that all the ribbons in one diagonal direction are placed first, then the others laid on top; rather than the two being woven through each other.

4 Embroider green straight stitches at the junctions of the ribbons, and cross stitches at the centre of each diamond. Then embroider pink cross stitches over the green cross stitches.

5 Machine- or hand-stitch a bias-cut strip of green silk to the perimeter of the padded base, right sides facing. Turn to cover raw edge and press lightly to hold in place. Stitch the padded base in place to cover the raw centre of the basket lining.

6 To make the lid: cut a piece of yellow silk and a piece of ivory silk to shape. Place the yellow on top of

an identical piece of wadding. Appliqué the ribbons and stitch the embroidery as for the padded liner.

7 Place the embroidered top right side facing to the ivory silk. Pin, baste and stitch together. Graduate seam allowances and clip curves. Turn right side out; slipstitch closed.

8 Stitch the fringed ribbon around the perimeter of face of lid, turning under raw edges where they meet.

9 Bind ribbon decoratively around basket handle, securing in place at either end with a few tiny stitches.

Shopping basket

This shopping basket was purchased in a wonderful specialist shop in Norwich, England. The basket has been in my family for generations, and has outlived many home-made fabric covers.

Made of full willow, rather than the less expensive and more brittle split willow of some modern versions, this very sturdy shopping basket is of timeless design. Unfortunately, baskets are no longer produced in the shop where this was bought, but well-made English full-willow baskets are still sold there – all faithful to the original designs.

Such baskets are not difficult to find, either new or old. It is worth investing in the best quality available. A good basket should feel smooth to the touch, with no jagged surfaces. Willow is the perfect material for baskets, and has not been bettered to this day. It is still used for everything from the baskets suspended beneath hot air balloons, which need to yield slightly as they land, to the humble shopping basket, which requires the same properties of strength, lightness of weight and flexibility.

Most willow baskets available today are of this warm buff colour, which works harmoniously with the cheerful gingham ribbon used to trim the calico cover. The wire edging has been removed from the ribbon, making the cover washable, and there is a practical elasticated opening in the middle, concealed beneath the ribbon frill, so that single items can be popped into the basket easily. The outer frill also conceals elastication, so that each side of the cover can be lifted up independently to accommodate larger items.

RIGHT With its wire edging removed, wide gingham craft ribbon adds a cheerful rustic flourish to a practical calico basket cover. Silk ribbon wrapped around the handle continues the lively colour theme.

ABILITY LEVEL
Intermediate

FINISHED SIZE
53 x 49cm/21 x 19¼in

RIBBONS
1 piece 2.3m/3yd (for the perimeter ruffle) 1 piece 1m/1yd (for the centre ruffle) of 7cm/3in-wide cotton gingham ribbon (wire removed if purchased with a wire edge)

[To calculate ribbon requirement for a different size of basket: you will need 2 times the perimeter measurement for the perimeter ruffle and 3 times the basket width across centre for the centre ruffle]

1m/1¼yd of 8mm/⅓in wide silk ribbon

50cm/20in of 2.5cm/½in-wide matt twill ribbon

TOOLS
Medium "Sharp" needle

Bodkin

FABRIC
2 pieces 25 x 42cm/10 x 16½in preshrunk first-quality calico, or sufficient to cover basket in two halves, one on each side of the handle, plus an additional 25% for seam allowances and wastage

OTHER MATERIALS
Cotton thread to match calico

Cotton thread to match ribbon

Willow shopping basket (available from Hovells of Norwich, England)

2m/2yd of 5mm/¼in elastic

STITCHES & TECHNIQUES
• Basic gathered ruffle
• Bow-tie bow
• Slip stitch
• Wrapping

MAKING UP
1 Fold over one long edge of each piece of fabric twice and machine stitch to make a 1.5cm/¾in-casing.

2 Using the bodkin, thread a separate length of elastic through each casing. Hand-stitch to fix the elastic firmly at one end. Lay each piece of the fabric across the centre of the basket and draw up the elastic within each casing until it is under a suitable tension to hold the fabric firmly in place.

3 Hand-stitch the tautened elastic securely in place at the remaining end of each casing.

4 With the fabric pieces still in position, mark the fabric around the perimeter of the basket with pins, indicating where the finished casing should sit. The casing here is fixed just below the basket rim.

5 Draw a line 3cm/1¼in outside the pinned line. Remove the fabric from the basket and cut to shape.

6 Fold over the shaped edge of each piece of fabric twice and machine-stitch to make a 1.5cm/¾in casing. Hand-stitch the two fabric pieces together where the casings join, leaving a channel through which to thread the elastic.

7 Machine-stitch a 1.5cm/½in seam to join the ribbon for the perimeter ruffle across its width. Press seam open.

8 Run a gathering stitch along one edge of the perimeter ribbon and draw up evenly until it forms a ruffle long enough to sit comfortably just inside the stitch line of the perimeter casing.

9 Hand-stitch the perimeter ruffle in place.

10 Run a gathering stitch along one edge of the centre ribbon and draw up evenly until it forms a ruffle long enough to sit comfortably across the basket, allowing a 3cm/1¼in double-turned hem at each end.

11 Hand-stitch the centre ruffle in place just inside the stitch line of one of the centre casings. Slipstitch hems at each end.

12 Using the bodkin, thread a single length of elastic through the perimeter casing. Draw up the elastic within the casing until it is under a suitable tension to hold the fabric firmly around the basket. Knot the tautened elastic securely.

13 Wrap the silk ribbon around the basket handle and tie off neatly at each end.

14 Make a bow-tie bow from the matt twill ribbon and attach by hand-stitching where the centre ruffle meets the perimeter ruffle.

ALTERNATIVE IDEAS

This simple treatment would be equally effective as a lid for a laundry basket – allowing linen to be placed inside through the elasticated gap, then concealed neatly beneath the calico.

Follow the directions for the shopping basket to make a template to fit any basket of your choice. Sewing baskets could also benefit from this decorative and practical idea.

BELOW This shopping basket, made of full willow, has been enhanced by the addition of gingham ribbon. The wire edging has been removed and there is a practical elasticated opening in the middle.

Coat hangers

Antique dealers often use padded coathangers to store and display old costumes. As well as providing a useful buffered surface for fragile garments, they are now collectable in their own right – adding an old-fashioned charm to a practical necessity.

From the 1930s, people made their own padding for hangers to protect their clothes; first in printed fabrics, later in plain satins, as has been done here. To decorate the utilitarian original, and hide the rather clumsy hand-stitching, I added a ribbon ruffle. This was achieved by running a gathering stitch centrally along a length of ribbon and drawing it up along the stitch until the ruffle was the correct length. This was then hand-stitched through each valley to attach the ruffle to the coathanger. The ruffle also helps to prevent clothes sliding off the hanger. The metal hook was also covered – in toning shades of old rose and lavender ribbon – and finished with a bow.

As a gesture to the period in which the original was created, a 1930s satin ribbon was used to make the lavender ruffle. This proved to be a very lucky find in an early-morning forage through a flea market in Bath, England. The ribbons were still in their original metal bands, and had obviously been stored in a haberdashers' window for years. All were faded to different degrees, making them perfect for adding the right note of worn elegance to the coathangers.

The delightfully floppy rayon tape of the lavender bow shows how well modern ribbons combine with old fabrics Contemporary colourings and weaves of ribbons are of such subtlety that old and new can be mixed with impunity.

RIGHT Old and new ribbons combine harmoniously on these coathangers to produce pretty and useful gifts.

Lavender sachets

With this selection of ribbon-threaded scented sachets made from dressing-table mats (originally known as Cheval sets), a taste for immaculate white linens can be indulged on an attainable scale. Fine silk ribbons add a delicate fragility to the crisp fabrics, but the more exuberant gleam of satin may be preferred. These sachets are machine-sewn to make strong seams that contain fillings well, but could equally be hand-stitched using a small backstitch.

The ribbons are added by hand, a process both mechanical and soothing. The sachets are an excellent portable project; requiring no special equipment or embroidery hoop. I whiled away a lengthy train journey contentedly threading ribbons, much to the bemusement of my fellow passengers.

The sachets are filled with a mixture of cottage garden herbs and flowers. Dried lavender, rosemary sprigs, and spearmint leaves, with their corresponding essential oils, are said to be moth-repellent, and scent drawers beautifully. To fix the fragrance, add powdered orris root to the scented plant material and leave to steep in a glass or china container for at least two weeks before using. The small square sachet edged with palest pink ribbon, filled with rose petals and rose essential oil, was made as a gift for a new baby girl, to scent drawers of baby clothes, and soothe a weary mother. The openwork sachet has a lavender filling and is finished with blue ribbons reminiscent of the ribbons threaded through Victorian broderie anglaise camisoles. This would be a pretty gift for a bride; the "something blue" of tradition, and perfect for storing with the bridal outfit as a scented reminder of a special day.

RIGHT   The palest, narrowest silk ribbons trace delicate patterns through broderie anglaise eyelets and lace on these lavender sachets.

Baby sachet

ABILITY LEVEL
Beginner

FINISHED SIZE
5 x 5cm/2 x 2in

RIBBONS
Narrow silk ribbon in palest blue or pink – width to suit eyelet holes in fabric x length of design to be threaded. [This sachet uses 3mm x 20cm/⅛in x 7¾in, plus 20cm/7¾in to tie off in a bow]

TOOLS
Bodkin with eye large enough to comfortably take ribbon

FABRIC
Scraps of white cotton or linen with eyelet holes in the design

OTHER MATERIALS
White cotton thread

Filling for pink sachet: dried rose petals scented with rose essential oil

Filling for blue sachet: dried marjoram scented with rosemary essential oil

STITCHES AND TECHNIQUES
• Buttonhole stitch
• Sewing with ribbon
• Simple tied bow
• Decorative threading

MAKING UP
1 Press the fabric so that it is square and even.

2 With wrong sides facing, and placing the eyelet design carefully, machine-embroider the front of the sachet to the back using a scalloped satin stitch (see page 18 in the *Before You Begin* section), leaving a small gap for filling. Alternatively, hand-stitch scallops in buttonhole stitch, marking out the design onto the fabric first.

3 Fill with flowers and continue stitching scallops to close.

4 Using the bodkin, thread the ribbon through the eyelet holes and finish with a bow.

5 Carefully trim away excess fabric from scalloped edge.

LEFT These lavender sachets have been beautifully enhanced by the addition of ribbons. Fine silk ribbons add a delicate fragility, but the more exuberant gleam of satin may be preferred.

Bride's sachet

ABILITY LEVEL
Beginner

FINISHED SIZE
9 x 6cm/3½ x 2⅜in

RIBBONS
Narrow silk ribbon in two shades
of pale blue – width to suit size of
holes x length of design to be
threaded.

[This sachet uses 4mm x 50cm/
¼ x 19½in and 5mm x 50cm/
¼ x 19½in, plus 60cm/23½in
of each colour to tie off in
decorative loops.]

TOOLS
Bodkin

Fine "Sharp" needle

FABRIC
Scraps of white cotton or
linen featuring drawn
threadwork through which to
thread ribbon.

OTHER MATERIALS
White cotton thread

Filling: lavender scented with
lavender essential oil

White muslin

Silk thread to match
the ribbons

STITCHES AND TECHNIQUES
• Buttonhole stitch
• Back stitch
• Sewing with ribbon
• Decorative threading
• Decorative looping

MAKING UP
1 Press the fabric so that it is
square and even.

2 With wrong sides facing,
machine-embroider the front
of the sachet to the back, using
a scalloped satin stitch; sandwich
the muslin in between, leaving
a small gap for filling. Alternatively,
you could hand-stitch the scallops in
buttonhole stitch, marking out the
design onto the fabric first.

3 Fill with lavender and continue
stitching scallops to close.

4 Using the bodkin, thread
the ribbon through the design.
It is important to control the
degree of twist carefully in order
to make a pleasing arrangement of
laid ribbons.

5 Combine the ends of the
ribbons in bows, and loop the
ends over and over decoratively.
Secure with tiny stitches in silk
thread.

6 Highlight a part of the design
with neat back-stitches in silk
thread, making the stitches not
quite as long as the ribbon is
wide. Take care to pass the needle
through only the top layer of
the sachet.

7 Using the bodkin, loop the ribbon
through the silk back-stitches. Snip
the loops.

8 Secure the snipped loops with
neat additional stitches in silk thread
if necessary.

9 Carefully trim away the excess
fabric from the scalloped edge.

Cheval mat sachet

ABILITY LEVEL
Beginner

FINISHED SIZE
19 x 19cm/7½ x 7½in

RIBBONS
Narrow silk ribbon in palest gray –
width to suit eyelet holes in fabric x
length of design to be threaded. This
sachet uses 3mm x 90cm/⅛ x 35⅛in,
plus 50cm/16½in to tie off in a bow

TOOLS
Bodkin

FABRIC
A pair of white dressing-table mats
with eyelet hole borders

OTHER MATERIALS
White cotton thread

Filling: dried lavender, rosemary and
spearmint, scented with appropriate
essential oils.

STITCHES AND TECHNIQUES
• Simple tied bow
• Sewing with ribbon

1 Press the fabric so that it is
square and even.

2 Wrong sides facing, machine- or
hand-stitch front of sachet to back,
using any motifs as a guide, or at a
distance from the edge appropriate
to your design; leave gap for filling.

3 Fill with herb mixture and
continue stitching to close.

4 With the bodkin, thread the
ribbon through the eyelet holes;
finish with a bow.

Heart sachets

Ribbons or fringed tapes were often stitched inside the trailing skirt hems that were popular during the late 19th and early 20th centuries. These false hems – known as dust ruffles or *balayeuses* – brushed smoothly over the ground, protecting the fabric of the garment.

In this rather more frivolous application, lengths of fringed tape have been folded in half by an innovative friend who owns an antique shop (Tobias and The Angel in London, England – see page 128) packed with delectable treasures such as these. They have then been stitched together and trimmed with rocaille beads, to produce a sumptuous double-edged braid.

These pretty hearts of silk damask and ticking are further embellished with short single lengths of the same tape, then gathered into attractive rosettes and finished off with faceted golden glass beads.

Hung over a wardrobe door handle, bedpost or dressing-table mirror, these sachets are a wonderfully romantic addition to a decorating scheme. Add a few drops of pure essential oil to the filling for a soothing scent. Rose, lavender, and geranium oils are particularly noted for their relaxing properties.

The satisfying plumpness of the trio of hearts comes from their carefully overstuffed centres – reminiscent of Victorian upholstery. Use a pencil to ensure that the filling reaches into every curve of the heart. It is important to stuff the point at the base of the heart well, so that it retains its shape in use.

RIGHT A length of tape, fringed on one side only, becomes an extravagant braid when layered with running stitches to produce a double-fringed edge. The single-fringed edge tape forms neat rosettes that conceal structural stitching.

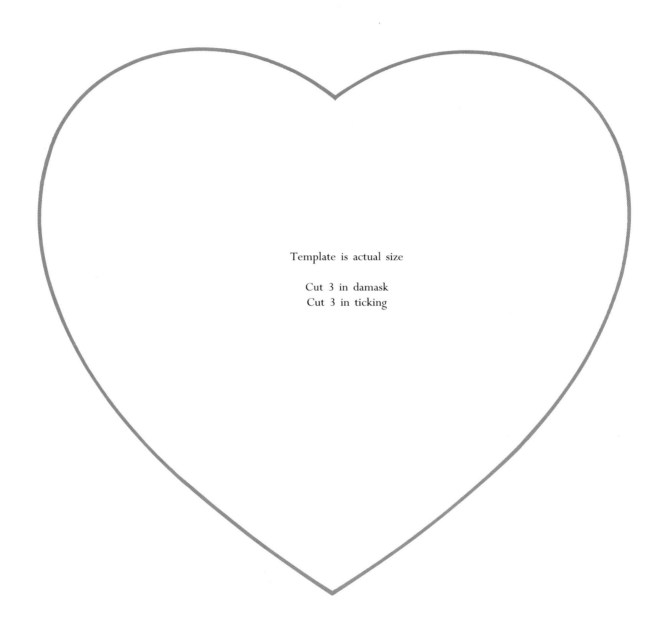

Template is actual size

Cut 3 in damask
Cut 3 in ticking

ABILITY LEVEL
Beginner

FINISHED SIZE
Each heart is approximately
12cm/4¾in diameter

RIBBONS
220cm/86½in of 2cm/¾in-wide
red fringed tape

TOOLS
Medium "Sharp" needle

Fine beading needle

FABRIC
1 piece of red/natural stripe
ticking 15cm x 45cm/
16 x 17¾in

1 piece of red damask
15cm x 45cm/16 x 17¾in

OTHER MATERIALS
80 pewter-coloured tiny round
glass beads (rocailles)

6 x faceted golden glass beads

105cm/41½in of red/black/
cream piping cord

Stuffing

Red silk thread

STITCHES AND TECHNIQUES
• Running stitch
• Slip stitch

MAKING UP
1 Press the fabrics so that they are
square and even.

2 Place the ticking on the damask,
with right sides facing. Transfer the
design (using the template on
page 112) onto the ticking three
times. Cut out three pairs of
heart shapes.

3 Pin, baste and stitch each pair
together – right sides facing – using
a 1.5cm/⅝in seam allowance. Leave
a small gap along one long edge of
each heart for turning.

4 Turn each heart right side out.
Stuff very firmly, and then slipstitch
the hearts closed.

5 Beginning at the top of each
heart, slipstitch piping cord around
the circumference to conceal the
seam, binding the ends neatly
with thread.

6 Cut lengths of fringed tape as
follows: the first length should
measure 32cm/12½in, the second
should be 52cm/20½in and the
third 72cm/28½in.

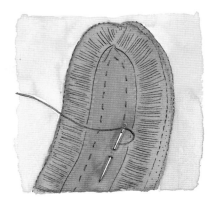

7 At the halfway point along the
length of each piece of fringed
tape make a 360 degree turn,
keeping the tape uppermost.
Place the left-hand piece of
fringed tape on top of the tape
that is now to your right, so
that the fringe protrudes evenly
on both sides (see above).

Do not fold. Take up the
excess tape in a neat tuck and
stitch to secure. Stitch the two
layers of tape together using
running stitch.

8 Stitch rocaille beads evenly
along the centre of each length of
layered tape.

9 Place the three layered lengths
of tape on a surface with the
longest first, graduating to the
shortest on top. Join the three
tapes together at the top by
stitching through all three tapes
approximately 5cm/2in from the
folded ends.

10 Fold under the raw end
of the longest tape twice, and
stitch firmly to the ticking at
the top of one of the hearts.
Repeat this step for the medium-
length, then the shortest tape,
adjusting the length of each
tape so that the tip of each heart
sits comfortably in the hollow of
its neighbour.

Rosettes
11 Make four rosettes as follows:
Firstly, gather a length of fringed
tape measuring 15cm/6in along
the unfringed edge. Pull up into a
rosette shape.

12 Stitch three of the rosettes
in place, to cover the joined ends
of the piping cord at the top of
each heart. Stitch a faceted gold
bead in the middle of each one.

13 Stitch the remaining rosette in
place to cover the stitch, joining
the three tapes together. Stitch
three faceted gold beads in the
middle of this final rosette.

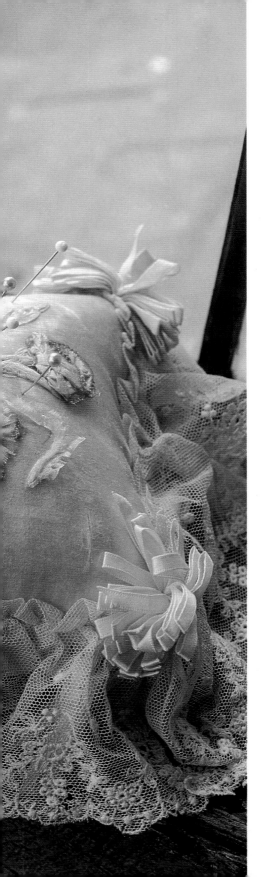

Pincushions

These sweet Victorian pincushions, in their sugar-almond colours, were kindly loaned by a friend who could hardly bear to let them out of her sight. They have been personal favourites for many years. The ribbons and lace are so fragile that they have an ethereal, almost spectral quality.

The forget-me-not design displays the Victorian passion for painting on satin, and also features the ribbon ruffles and rosettes which appeared on everything from fashionable garments to home furnishings in this period.

The larger of the two pincushions features some very simple ribbon-embroidered carnations. Carnations were a favourite subject for ribbon embroidery. Their pinked edges and ruffled shape makes them ideally suited to the medium. Special ribbons with serrated, or picotee, edges were manufactured to make the effect even more realistic.

Decorative pincushions such as those shown here were created as much for adding an opulent touch to a dressing table, as for purely practical reasons.

There is some debate as to the optimum filling for pincushions. Variously, sawdust, emery powder, iron filings, bran and wool have all been used. I would recommend perfectly dry sawdust, or natural wool – these are the fillings that have been specified for this project. Scraps of used knitting or tapestry wool could also acquire a new lease of life, used in this way. I find that synthetic fillings are difficult to pack sufficiently tightly to give a well-padded surface that holds pins securely.

LEFT Faded to watercolour paleness, the silk, satin and ombré ribbons used in a variety of techniques on these pincushions epitomize the sentimental prettiness of most Victorian ribbonwork.

Forget-me-not pincushion

ABILITY LEVEL
Intermediate

FINISHED SIZE
Approximately 13 x 13cm/
5 x 5in

RIBBONS
13mm/½in-wide x
3m/3¼yd pale blue ombré
silk ribbon – for edging
the perimeter of the
ruffle

5mm/¼in x 1m/1¼yd-
wide pale blue silk ribbon
– to cover the point where
the ruffle joins the pincushion

5mm/¼ x 50cm/19¾in-
wide white silk ribbon –
both for trimming the
interior edge of the ruffle and
forming the rosettes

1 piece of white silk
jacquard ribbon approximately
7cm/2¾in deep x 1.5m/
1¾yd for the ruffle

TOOLS
Medium "Sharp" needle

Fine paintbrush

FABRIC
Two pieces of closely woven
white cotton for inner case;
each measuring 16 x 16cm/
6¼ x 6¼in

Two pieces of white
satin for outer cover,
each measuring 16 x 16cm/
6¼ x 6¼in

OTHER MATERIALS
Dry sawdust or natural wool
for filling

White silk thread

Pale blue silk thread

Fabric paints

STITCHES AND TECHNIQUES
• Painting and dyeing
• Gathering

MAKING UP
1 Press the fabrics so that they
are square and even. Transfer
the design onto the face of
one of the satin squares.
Use the template provided
on the following page and
reduce to 90%.

2 Place the satin squares
together, with right sides
facing, sandwiched between
the two squares of lining
fabric (the closely woven
white cotton). Pin, baste and
machine-stitch together using
white silk thread, leaving a gap
for turning and stuffing.

3 Turn the satin and the lining
fabric right side out and stuff
(using the dry sawdust or natural
wool) as firmly as possible. Stitch
the layers closed.

The ruffle
4 Run a gathering stitch
centrally along the length
of the narrow pale blue ombré
ribbon (see the illustration above).
Draw up the ribbon to form
an even ruffle – this should
be the same length as the jacquard
ribbon. Then stitch the ruffle in

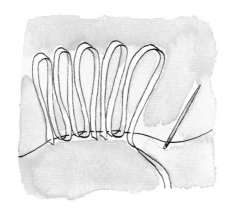

place along one edge of the
jacquard ribbon. Stitch together
the short ends of the trimmed
jacquard ribbon – with right
sides facing – to form a circle.
Press the seam open.

5 Run a gathering stitch
along the remaining long
edge of the ribbon measuring
7cm/2¾in.

6 Stitch the gathered ribbon
neatly onto the face of the
pincushion (see the illustration) –
following the lines on the
pattern. Make sure that you
allow a sufficient quantity of
ribbon to make a generous
frill at each corner.

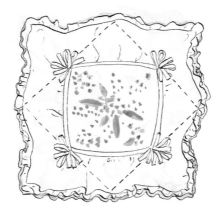

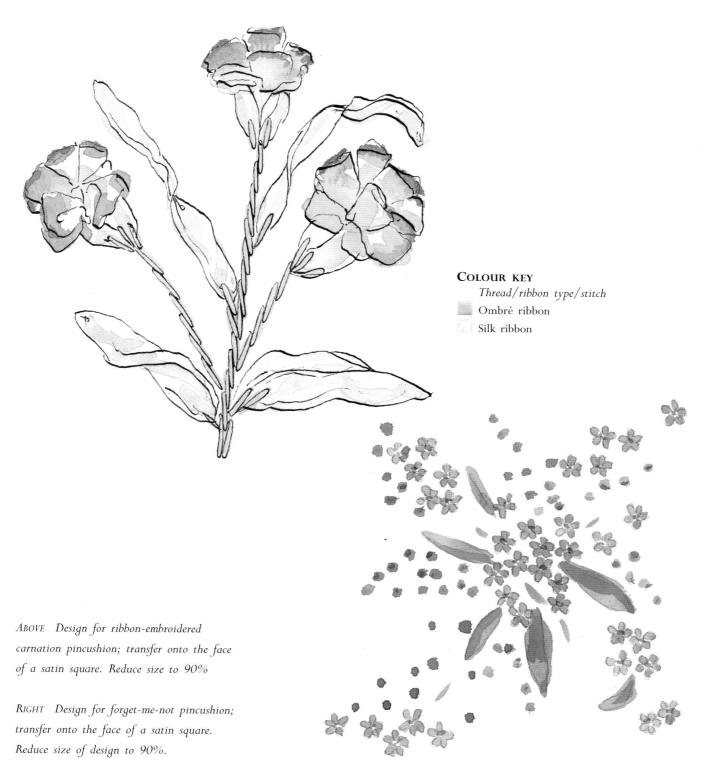

COLOUR KEY
Thread/ribbon type/stitch
Ombré ribbon
Silk ribbon

ABOVE Design for ribbon-embroidered
carnation pincushion; transfer onto the face
of a satin square. Reduce size to 90%

RIGHT Design for forget-me-not pincushion;
transfer onto the face of a satin square.
Reduce size of design to 90%.

7 Paint the forget-me-not design (see page 115) onto the centre of the pincushion. Fix according to the manufacturer's instructions.

8 When the fabric paint is thoroughly dried and fixed, you should then place the 5mm/¼in-wide blue ribbon so that it covers the point at which the ruffle joins the pincushion. Stitch this ribbon in place at each point of the square, where the rosettes will be attached.

Rosettes

9 To make each rosette, fold a 15cm/5in length of narrow blue ribbon back and forth – concertina style – onto a needle threaded with silk making even folds in the ribbon, spaced approximately 2.5cm/1in apart. Leave the needle threaded, and repeat this step using a 15cm/5in length of narrow white ribbon – folded and threaded onto the same piece of thread, making a pink and white rosette on completion. When both colours have been folded and threaded to form a rosette, secure each one with small backstitches before stripping off the thread end.

10 Stitch each rosette in place.

Carnation pincushion

SKILL LEVEL
Beginner

FINISHED SIZE
Approximately 27 x 27cm/10½ x 10½in including the ruffle

RIBBONS
Pink silk ombré ribbon measuring 13mm/½in wide, for embroidering the carnations

White silk ribbon measuring 7mm/¼in-wide for embroidering the leaves

5mm/¼in-wide x 3m/3¼yd white woven-edge double-faced silk ribbon for the rosettes at the corners

5mm/¼in-wide x 3m/3¼yd palest pink woven-edge double-faced silk ribbon for the rosettes at the corners

A piece of palest pink silk or woven-edge satin ribbon measuring approximately 6.5cm/2½in deep x 1.5m/1¾yd for ruffle

TOOLS
Medium "Sharp" needle for silk thread

Crewel needle for ribbon embroidery

FABRIC
Two pieces of closely woven white cotton for the inner case, each measuring 16 x 16cm/ 6¼ x 6¼in

Two pieces of white satin for the outer cover – each measuring 16 x 16cm/6¼ x 6¼in

OTHER MATERIALS
A piece of lace measuring approx. 7cm/2 ¾in deep x 1.5m/1¾yd

Stranded embroidery cotton in pale green for stems [use three strands DMC 966/Anchor 206]

Pale pink silk thread

White silk thread

Dry sawdust or natural wool for filling

STITCHES AND TECHNIQUES
• Stem stitch
• Gathering
• Sewing with ribbon
• Making flowers
• Painting and dyeing

MAKING UP

1 Press the fabrics so that they are square and even. Transfer the design (a template has been provided on page 115 to help you plot the design; reduce pattern to 90%) onto the face of one of the satin squares.

2 Work the thread embroidery using the pale green stranded cotton, followed by the ribbon embroidery, using the pink ombré and white silk ribbons.

The carnations
To form each carnation, take a 30.5cm/12in length of 13mm/½in pink ombré ribbon. Stitch the short ends together, with right sides facing. Run a gathering stitch around one long edge of the ribbon. Pull up tightly to form a circular ruffle. Stitch to secure. Stitch in place,

holding down the ribbon with tiny silk thread stitches to form some open flowers and some profile flowers, referring to the photograph (on page 113) as a guide.

Single twist leaf
To form a single twist leaf, bring the ribbon up through fabric and extend it to the required length of the leaf — twisting the ribbon once before taking it back through the fabric. Invisibly stitch the twist in place by securing in the crease.

3 Place the embroidered satin and plain satin squares together — with right sides facing — sandwiched between the two squares of lining fabric. Pin, baste, and machine-stitch together using white silk thread, leaving a gap for turning and stuffing.

4 Turn right side out and stuff (using dry sawdust or natural wool) as firmly as possible. Stitch closed.

5 Stitch together the short ends of the piece of 7cm/2¾in-wide ribbon, with right sides facing. Press the seam open. Run a

gathering stitch along one long edge of the ribbon. Stitch neatly to perimeter of pincushion, just covering the seam, allowing plenty of ribbon to make a generous frill at each corner.

6 Stitch together the short ends of the piece of lace — with right sides facing — and press the seam open. Run a gathering stitch along one long edge of the lace. Now stitch this neatly to perimeter of pincushion, just covering where the ribbon ruffle joins the pincushion. You should allow sufficient lace at each corner to form a generous frill, as for the ribbon ruffle.

Rosettes
7 To make each rosette, fold a 72cm/28¼in length of narrow pink ribbon back and forth concertina style onto a needle threaded with silk thread. Make even folds, spaced 3cm/1in apart. Continue folding and threading on the white ribbon.

8 Stitch a rosette in place at each corner of the pincushion.

ADAPTING THE DESIGN
The forget-me-not and carnation designs would be equally suited for application to a larger, conventional cushion cover. Simply scale-up the designs and ribbon width until they are appropriate to your finished cushion size.

Alternatively, scatter tiny floral motifs over a larger cushion for a delicate, romantic feel. Make the cover removable for laundering by securing with ribbon ties, snap fasteners or a zip.

Shoe trees

A scrap of irresistible 18th-century fabric, unearthed in a country antiques shop, was the inspiration for these glamorous and practical shoe trees. They would be a perfect gift for a bride – perhaps made in scraps of fabric and ribbons used in the making of the wedding dress.

The finished shoe trees are wonderfully tactile, using narrow silk ribbons to great effect in many different ways; as three-dimensional embroidery, to form a crisp ruffle around the throat of the handle, and as a smooth wrapping for the stem. They are almost too pretty to tuck inside shoes. Although they may be created with the intention of becoming a gift, you may find them difficult to part with.

The foam shoe trees beneath the sumptuously trimmed covers are inexpensive and widely available, and form a luxurious cushioned base for the embroidered fabric. Alternatively, old wooden shoe trees could be trimmed in the same way – by adding a layer of wadding before applying the calico liner.

Silk ribbon has just the right amount of tensile spring to move happily in accordance with the metal tensioner. It is available in the most delightfully subdued period-style colours – known, rather unromantically, as "drabs". I was thrilled to find that the exact shade of faded willow-green, mulberry and damask-rose silk ribbons I had imagined using for this project are still being manufactured today. The natural tones of these ribbons recall early plant dyes of lichen, mosses and roots, and complement old fabrics beautifully. They also add a touch of antiquated charm to reproduction textiles, such as the contemporary cotton *toile* used on the soles of the shoe trees.

RIGHT Too pretty to tuck inside shoes, these silk ribbon-trimmed shoe trees are decorative enough to display in their own right.

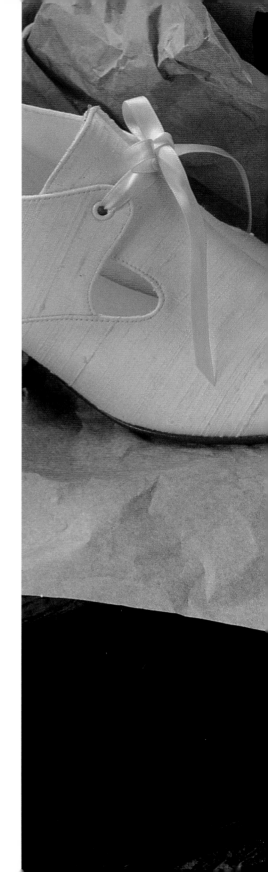

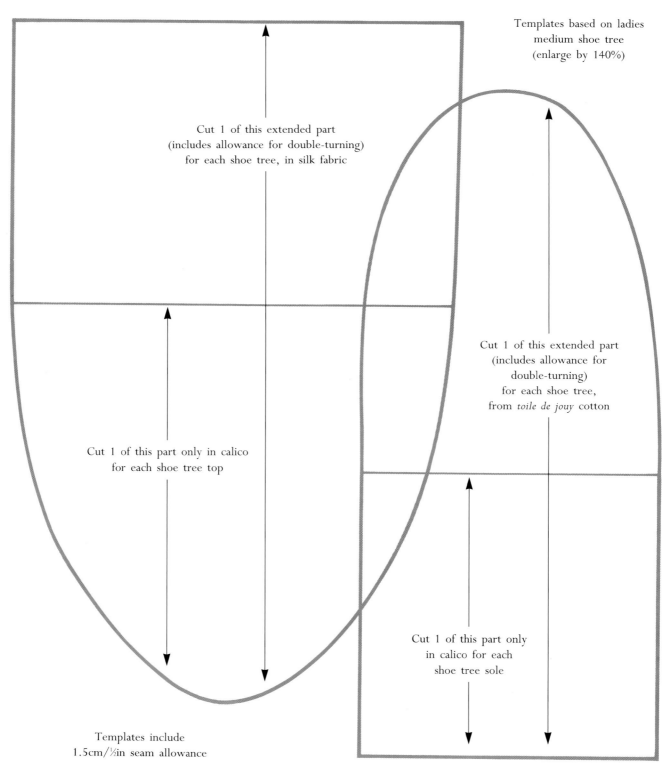

Templates based on ladies
medium shoe tree
(enlarge by 140%)

Cut 1 of this extended part
(includes allowance for double-turning)
for each shoe tree, in silk fabric

Cut 1 of this extended part
(includes allowance for
double-turning)
for each shoe tree,
from *toile de jouy* cotton

Cut 1 of this part only in calico
for each shoe tree top

Cut 1 of this part only
in calico for each
shoe tree sole

Templates include
1.5cm/⅝in seam allowance

ABILITY LEVEL Beginner

FINISHED SIZE
Make to suit individual shoe size.
[Sizes and amounts are approximate
as each individual shoe size will
make a slight difference]

RIBBONS
Approx. 3m/3¼yd of 13mm/½in
width burgundy silk ribbon for stems

Approx. 3m/3¼yd of 7mm/¼in
width damask-rose silk ribbon to
form ruffles

Approx. 1m/1yd of 4mm/⅛in width
burgundy silk ribbon to whip the
running stitch embroidery

Approx. 1m/1yd of 2mm/⅛in width
willow-green silk ribbon for running
stitch embroidery

Approx 1.5m/1½yd of 4mm/⅛in
width willow-green silk ribbon for
tied bows

TOOLS
Crewel needle for ribbon
embroidery; medium "Sharp" needle
for silk thread

FABRIC
1 piece of silk fabric approx. 26 x
45cm/10¼ x 17¾in for decorative
fronts and handle ends of shoe trees

1 piece of *toile de jouy* printed cotton
fabric approx. 26 x 32cm/
10¼ x 12½in for soles of shoe trees

1 piece of calico 16 x 2cm/6¼ x
20½in for making the liner

OTHER MATERIALS
Shoe trees (available from most shoe
shops and department stores)

Neutral-coloured silk thread

Pencil or fade-out fabric marker

MAKING UP
1 Press the fabrics so that they are
square and even.

2 Draw around foot part of shoe
tree onto paper, bringing paper
around the sole, up to where handle
is attached. Wrap a second piece of
paper around top of the foot part.
Mark on the paper where this piece
meets the sole of the shoe tree.

3 Add 1.5cm/⅝in seam allowance
outside each pattern piece and draw
in place to form cutting template.
Add 10cm/5in at line shown on the
pattern piece for surface fabric,
sufficient to make double turning
that is tied off with a bow.

4 Transfer the templates as
follows: each shoe tree requires
one top in calico, one in surface
fabric and one sole in calico, one in
surface fabric.

5 For each shoe tree, place a calico
top on a calico sole right sides
facing, matching the edges. Pin,
baste and stitch together around the
lines indicated, pinning the excess
fabric to itself along the centre to
keep it out of the way while you
stitch. Turn right side out. Press
seam open and clip curves. Place on
shoe tree form. Pull tightly to fit.
Pin, then stitch firmly in place.

6 Work ribbon embroidery on top
piece of surface fabric for each shoe
tree. Stitch a row of running stitch
in 2mm/⅛in width willow-green silk
ribbon at the lines indicated (see
illustration). Whip 4mm/³⁄₁₆in-width

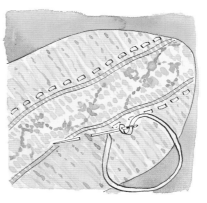

burgundy silk ribbon through each
line of ribbon stitch, so whipping
stitches lie at full width comfortably
on surface of fabric. Wrap stem of
each shoe tree with the 13mm/½in
width burgundy silk ribbon. Secure
at each end with tiny stitches.

7 Cut a circle of surface fabric of
sufficient size to wrap around the
end of each handle. Run a gathering
stitch around the edge of each circle.
Draw up to fit and stitch securely in
place, tucking raw edges inside.

8 Ribbon ruffle around collar of each
handle: run a gathering stitch along
one long edge of a piece of damask-
rose ribbon 7mm/¼in wide x 1.5m/
1.5yd long. Pull tight. Wrap around
handle and secure with tiny stitches.

9 Place embroidered piece on a sole
piece, right sides facing, matching
edges. Pin together, pinning the
excess fabric out of the way along
the centre before stitching the pieces
together. Press seams open and clip
curves. Turn right side out and place
on shoe tree form; then fold excess
fabric toward the inside of the shoe
tree twice, to conceal all raw edges.

10 Stitch neck of shoe tree securely
closed. Add a simple tied bow.

Needlecase

This enchanting needlecase was made at the turn of the century. The skill of working with ribbons on a very small scale is particularly impressive here. The rolled cones of fine silk gauze ribbon are secured by stitches of silk thread so dainty as to be barely visible to the naked eye.

It is very difficult to obtain narrow silk gauze ribbon today, and synthetic organdy will not give anything like the same delicate result. To mimic either I have experimented with carefully removing alternate weft threads from silk ribbon. This produces a very pretty result, but is certainly a labour of love. The resulting gauzy ribbon is rather fragile, although you can stiffen it following one of the sizeing suggestions in the *Before You Begin* section (see page 16) of this book. Alternatively, create the rolled cones from plain silk ribbon.

The needlecase also features floss silk, chenille thread, and ombré ribbon. Late 18th-century floral designs such as this were often worked in myriad combinations of textures for a delightfully varied result. The effect is extremely pretty – reminiscent of *millefiori*, "thousand flowers" glass designs.

Numerous stitches are included on this needlecase – slip, stem and French knots to name but a few – making it an ideal project on which to practise your needlwork skills. On the following pages we have provided a plan of the floral design on the needlecase. Reduce this to 33%.

LEFT The brilliant colours and diminutive scale of the embroidery on this needlecase give a jewel-like sparkle to the design. It demonstrates the skill involved in working with ribbons on a very small scale.

ABILITY LEVEL
Intermediate

FINISHED SIZE
15.5 x 11cm/6 x 4½in

RIBBONS
Scraps of 2mm/¹⁄₁₆in silk ribbon in a selection of subtle colours (selection packs from dolls' house mail order companies are perfect)

Colours to include subdued, period-style shades of pink, blue, white, green, apricot, yellow, brown, in varied tones

Scraps of 5mm/⅛in organdy ribbon (ideally silk), in shades of taupe and pink

14cm/5½in of 7mm/¼in brown silk ribbon for spine of needlecase

TOOLS
Crewel needle

Fine "Sharp" needle

pinking shears

FABRIC
1 piece of fine brown silk
18 x 14cm/7 x 5½in

3 pieces of lightweight flannel each
14 x 10cm/5½ x 4in (cut out using pinking shears)

1 piece of calico 17.5 x 12.5cm/
6¾ x 5¼in

OTHER MATERIALS
Brown silk thread

Scraps of stranded embroidery cotton in shades of green, brown, pink, golden yellow (use two strands)

Scraps of silk thread in shades of green, brown, blue, yellow and pale pink

Scraps of chenille thread in shades of green, brown, taupe and yellow

Scraps of embroidery floss in shades of green (use two strands)

STITCHES AND TECHNIQUES
• Straight stitch
• Slip stitch
• Stem stitch
• Pistil stitch
• Lazy-daisy stitch
• French knots
• Sewing with ribbon
• Rolled cones
• Making flowers
• Painting and dyeing
• Sizeing

MAKING UP
1 Press the silk so that it is square and even.

2 Transfer the design (on opposite page. Reduce to 33%).

3 Embroider the design, beginning with the stems, worked in silk thread. Embroider the ribbon stitches next, followed by the remaining silk thread, chenille, stranded embroidery cotton, and floss stitches.

4 Press a 1.5cm/½in seam allowance around the perimeter of the work, toward the wrong side. Press a 1.5cm/½in seam allowance around the perimeter of the calico.

5 Place the pieces of pinked-edged flannel on top of the calico, and then on top of the embroidered silk, with wrong sides facing. Backstitch through all the layers, forming a book.

6 Slipstitch the 7mm/¼in brown ribbon to the spine of the needlecase, tucking the raw ends between the calico and the silk. Slipstitch the calico lining to the silk.

COLOUR KEY
Thread/ribbon type/stitch
2mm/¹⁄₁₆in silk ribbon; straight
Ombré silk ribbon; lazy daisy
silk gauze ribbon; rolled cones
silk gauze ribbon; rolled cones
Chenille thread; straight stitch
Chenille thread; straight stitch
Chenille thread; straight stitch
Ombré ribbon; straight stitch
Leaves; straight/silk thread stem
Silk thread; pistil stitch/Fr.knot
Embroidery thread; Fr. knot

Index

Acknowledgements

Thanks to all the people who loaned pieces from their personal collections, supplied wonderful antique and contemporary ribbons as well as enthusiastically contributing to the historical research: Angel Hughes at Tobias and the Angel, Annabel Lewis at V.V. Rouleaux, Janet Bridge and Jen Jones at Jen Jones Antiques, Victoria's Antiques of Bath, Trish and Tony Longcraine, Stephen Lunn at Lunn Antiques, Dawn Lockyer, The Stuffed Dog Antiques and Joanna Proops Antiques.

Many thanks to the following people who were also invaluable in my research into the history and techniques of ribboncrafts: Graham Spedding of The Dollshouse Draper, Anna Pearson, John Jones at The Museum of The Welsh Woollen Industry, Steff Francis, Christine Stevens at The Welsh Folk Museum, Caroline Hamilton (organiser of the London Dollshouse Festival), The Victoria and Albert Museum and The Embroiderer's Guild. Thanks also to the Cutforth family, who displayed remarkable tolerance and good humour whilst we took over their home for much of the photographic shoot. To Don Reeve, Michael Gray, and the ladies at the Merchants House, Marlborough, for their hospitality during photography, and loan of props from The Merchants House shop. Thanks to the following people who loaned props for photography, in addition to those already mentioned: Brocante of Marlborough, Judy Greenwood Antiques, Cavendish House Antiques, Marlborough Parade Antiques Centre, Wedding Belles of Marlborough, Cross Hayes Antiques, Malmesbury, Old Town Antiques, Swindon, Wiltshire. Thanks to the following people who supplied ribbons and materials, Jersey Lavender, The Dollshouse Draper, The Natural Fabric Company, Ribbon Designs.

Thanks to the following suppliers: Jen Jones Antiques, Pontbrendu, Llanybydder, Dyfed, Wales; Judy Greenwood Antiques 657, Fulham Road, London SW6; Wedding Belles of Marlborough, 47 Kingsbury Street, Marlborough, Wiltshire; Cavendish House Antiques, 138 High Street, Marlborough, Wiltshire; Ribbon Designs, 42 Lake View, Edgware, Middlesex HA8 7RU; The Dollshouse Draper, PO Box 128 Lightcliffe, Halifax West Yorkshire HX3 8RN; V.V. Rouleaux, 10 Symons St, London SW3 2TJ; Tobias and The Angel, 68 White Hart Lane, Barnes, London SW13 0PZ; Cross Hayes Antiques, 19 Bristol Street, Malmesbury, Wiltshire; The Merchant's House, 132 High Street, Marlborough, Wiltshire, SN8; Joanna Proops Antiques; Victoria's Antiques, The Gallery, Bartlett Street Antiques Centre, Bath, Avon; Old Town Antiques, 17, Wood Street, Swindon, Wiltshire; Marlborough Parade Antiques Centre, The Parade, Marlborough, Wiltshire; The Natural Fabric Company, Wessex Court, High Street, Hungerford, Berkshire; Jersey Lavender Ltd, Rue du Pont Marquet, St. Brelade, Jersey, Channel Islands; The Museum of The Welsh Woollen Industry, Dre-Fach Felindre, Landysul, Dyfed, Wales SA54; The Welsh Folk Museum, St. Fagans, Cardiff, Wales CF5 6XB; Brocante, 6 London Road, Marlborough, Wiltshire; Trish and Tony Longcraine Antiques, 4 London Road, Marlborough, Wiltshire; The Embroiderer's Guild, Apartment 41, Hampton Court Palace, East Molesey, Surrey KT8 9AU; The Victoria and Albert Museum, Cromwell Road, South Kensington, London SW7 2RL; Lunn Antiques Ltd, 86 New King's Road, London SW6 4LU; Dawn Lockyer, Devon; The Stuffed Dog Antiques.

Many thanks to Tim Imrie and his assistant Faye Pattinson for consistently beautiful photography and endless patience. Thanks to Val Fullick, Martin Mansfield and Tony Hayes for moral support, encouragement and advice. Not least, I would like to thank my husband Andrew, for his involvement, interest, and support in every way.

Wiltshire, January 1996.